the best of
Terrie Lee Steinmeyer

Cross stitchers everywhere will be delighted with this comprehensive collection of designs by Terrie Lee Steinmeyer! Gathered from popular Leisure Arts publications, these perennial favorites include holiday, inspirational, baby, children, sports, and school themes—more than 140 projects! Make quick gifts like bookmarks, jar lid inserts, or Christmas ornaments. Fashion lovely keepsakes such as birth announcements and Mother's Day gifts. These designs are the best of the best, and will be cherished by your loved ones for years to come.

LEISURE ARTS, INC.
Little Rock, Arkansas

LEISURE ARTS EDITORIAL STAFF
Editor-in-Chief: Susan White Sullivan
Designer Relations Director: Debra Nettles
Craft Publications Director: Cheryl Johnson
Special Projects Director: Susan Frantz Wiles
Senior Prepress Director: Mark Hawkins

TECHNICAL
Technical Writers: Frances Huddleston, Mary Sullivan
  Hutcheson, Lisa Lancaster, and Jean Lewis
Editorial Writer: Susan McManus Johnson

ART
Art Publications Director: Rhonda Shelby
Art Category Manager: Lora Puls
Lead Graphic Artist: Janie Marie Wright
Graphic Artists: Dayle Carozza, Jacob Casleton,
  Angela Ormsby Stark, and Dana Vaughn
Imaging Technicians: Brian Hall,
  Stephanie Johnson, and Mark R. Potter
Publishing Systems Administrator: Becky Riddle
Publishing Systems Assistants: Clint Hanson
  and John Rose

BUSINESS STAFF
Vice President and Chief Operations Officer:
  Tom Siebenmorgen
Director of Finance and Administration:
  Laticia Mull Dittrich
Vice President, Sales and Marketing: Pam Stebbins
National Accounts Director: Martha Adams
Sales and Services Director: Margaret Reinold
Information Technology Director: Hermine Linz
Controller: Francis Caple
Vice President, Operations: Jim Dittrich
Comptroller, Operations: Rob Thieme
Retail Customer Service Manager: Stan Raynor
Print Production Manager: Fred F. Pruss

Library of Congress Control Number 2009934617
ISBN-13: 978-1-60140-592-0
ISBN-10: 1-60140-592-8

10 9 8 7 6 5 4 3 2 1

We have made every effort to ensure that these instructions are accurate and complete. We cannot, however, be responsible for human error, typographical mistakes, or variations in individual work.

table of

contents

the designer Terrie Lee Steinmeyer

"All my interests are related to each other, whether it's gardening, sketching, photography, 3D design on my computer, or sculpting. They all nourish my creative muse. I'm also just very grateful to the wonderful friends who have enjoyed my designs and who share my love of stitching."

"The people I have met through designing needlework have the biggest hearts," exclaims Terrie Lee Steinmeyer. "They are so excited about the projects they make for themselves, a sister, mother, friend, or new baby. For me, designing a baby ensemble is an unimaginably fun experience, but to know someone is stitching it for a loved one is incredibly fulfilling!"

Cross stitchers have been creating gifts from Terrie Lee's designs for more than twenty years. The Bucks County, Pennsylvania resident holds a degree in fine art. She enjoys painting with oils and sculpting, however, it was her watercolor illustrations that were the key to landing her first sales to a needlecraft company.

"It was a wonderful introduction to all forms of needlework, and the start of my lifelong love of cross stitching," Terrie Lee says. "I've also sold illustrations that became musical figurines, greeting cards, and holiday décor. I positively adore designing Christmas, Halloween, and Baby items. I believe that if you are lucky enough to love your work, it no longer feels like work."

Not satisfied to rest on the laurels of her past successes, the artist is still finding new ways to express her talent. "Recently," she says, "I have taken all the things that bring me joy and started creating one-of-a-kind dolls. They can be seen on my blog at www.rosielane.blogspot.com. I hope to teach doll making soon, both online and at workshops."

Terrie Lee's love of gardening is proving to be a help in this new endeavor. She says, "Growing gourds for my doll art is a blast! This year, the vines are threatening to cover the house.

"All my interests are related to each other," she continues, "whether it's gardening, sketching, photography, 3D design on my computer, or sculpting. They all nourish my creative muse. I'm also just very grateful to the wonderful friends who have enjoyed my designs and who share my love of stitching."

When asked what words of encouragement she has for newcomers to the world of cross stitch, she says, "When you are stitching a bookmark or bib for someone you care for, it's exciting! Whether you've been stitching for years or just a month, making a gift for that special someone is what cross stitch is all about!"

Sweet & Easy for Baby

Just for the nursery, here are a baby-block birth sampler, jar band, and door pillow in easy cross stitch. If you can't find cross stitch ribbon for the jar band, cut a piece of Aida cloth and sew rickrack or satin ribbon to the edges. Chart is on page 79.

5

Oh, Baby!

Here's a bevy of bright gift ideas for Baby—bibs, framed pieces, a door pillow, and a tote bag. They're highlighted with birds, bunnies, hearts, and other sweet motifs that let everyone know how much the little one is loved. Charts are on pages 98-104 and 106-108.

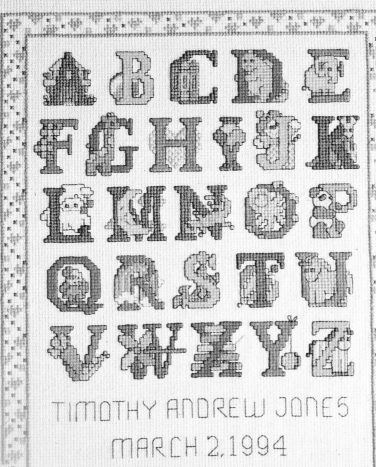

Precious Keepsakes

Choose from two wonderful ways to welcome Baby into the world. The alphabet birth announcement offers a variety of colorful animals and objects that the little tyke will enjoy naming as he grows older. The precious "Birth Certificate" announcement will remind everyone of Baby's early days. Be sure to use a non-toxic, water-based craft paint to capture the infant's footprints. Charts are on pages 96-97 and 105.

Children's Alphabets

Toy train and ice cream alphabets are a playful way to cross stitch a monogram or a favorite phrase. Stitch someone's initials on a patch of even-weave fabric to personalize a backpack or tote bag. Frame a youngster's name to put on a bedroom door. You'll think of many ways to stitch and display theses fun alphabets! Charts are on pages 91-95.

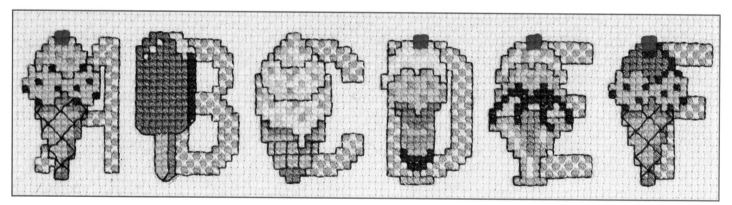

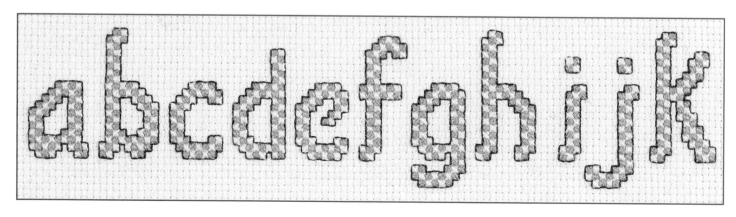

Put a (Fun) Lid on it!

For a thoughtful way to present any little gift—top a jar with a cross-stitched lid insert. This collection of 20 designs covers a wide variety of occasions. Charts are on pages 36-39.

Holiday House

What's the quickest way to decorate for holidays and special occasions? Create a cross stitch holiday house with 18 tiny celebration motifs to place on its door! Once the stitching's done, you'll be able to change the theme of this framed piece in just seconds. Charts are on pages 40-43.

At Your Fingertips

For gifts, for decorating, or just for fun, these 12 holiday towels put the celebration at your fingertips. Charts are on pages 44-47.

Valentine's Day

Here's a cute little cupid, ready to inspire loving thoughts for St. Valentine's Day. What a sweet reminder to set aside time for that special someone!

St. Patrick's Day

You'll enjoy the luck of the Irish when you wear the colors of the national flag of Ireland on your shirt pocket or a pair of pins with familiar Irish symbols. There's even a fingertip towel with a friendly saying to help you start the day.

Charts are on pages 48-50

INDEPENDENCE DAY

Show your true colors with a July 4th T-shirt. Waste canvas makes it possible to work counted cross stitch on almost any lightweight fabric.

Easter

Help the Easter Bunny paint colorful eggs on a fingertip towel and framed piece. The sweet designs are so heartwarming, it may be difficult to put them away when the holiday is over.

Charts are on pages 50-52.

HALLOWEEN

Candy corn, ghosts, pumpkins, and a friendly witch's cat get your Halloween celebration off to an eerily fun start! Charts are on pages 53-55.

Autumn, Thanksgiving, Christmas, & Winter

In fall and winter, there's just so much to be thankful for: Autumn, with all its beauty. Thanksgiving, that memorable day we gather to count our blessings. Christmas, the joyful season of giving and sharing. And winter, with its frozen splendor that brings out the kid in each of us! Charts are on pages 56-60.

Vintage Santas

Santa Claus, Père Noël, Kris Kringle—these Santas are the vintage variety, representing the kindly soul who tramped through woods and over hills to bring gifts to good children of the nineteenth century. Charts are on pages 61-64.

Ornaments for Tree & More

Great projects for beginning stitchers, these Christmas tree ornaments are also fun to tie on packages for gift-giving! Charts are on pages 66-69.

Praying Hands

German artist Albrecht Dürer´s brush drawing *Praying Hands* has inspired generations of faithful with its simple messages of dedication and sacrifice. It is told that a friend or brother of Dürer worked as a miner to put Dürer through art school, and it is this good friend or brother whose work-weary hands are the model for the artwork. Terrie Lee Steinmeyer´s adaptation captures the graceful image from Dürer's famous artistry. Chart is on page 65.

Keep Your Place

Whether reading for inspiration or relaxation, every fan of the written word could use a new bookmark—especially one that's stitched with love! Charts are on pages 70-74.

School Days & Sports

Get back to school with these fun projects that honor Teacher and the importance of learning. And if you know a sports nut, be sure he or she has a nice towel honoring their avocation! Charts are on pages 82-87.

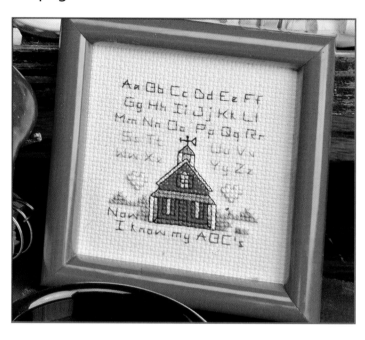

Carousel Ponies

As long as little girls love carousels, there will be a place for these pretty ponies to call home. Create a lovely framed piece or a ruffled pillow to brighten the life of a special young miss. Charts are on pages 88-89.

Take Note

These six fun magnets will help you keep track of artwork, shopping lists, and other important papers you post on the fridge. They're also nice for brightening up a workspace! Charts are on page 90.

ELLIOTT

You got it from your Father
it was all he had to give
So it's yours to use and cherish
for as long as you may live.

If you lost the watch he gave you
it can always be replaced;
but a black mark on your name
can never be erased.

It was clean the day you took it
and a worthy name to bear
when he got it from his Father
there was no dishonor there.

So make sure you guard it wisely
after all is said and done.
You'll be glad the name is spotless
when you give it to your son.

MOTHER

A Mother is one who can
take the place of all others,
but whose place no one
else can take.

Aunt
I wish you
all God's blessings
because, in all ways,
you have blessed
my life.

Because You Care

Mother, father, aunt, and friend—honor them always with these sweet designs! Create a framed piece, pillow, or box lid insert that tells these special people how important they are to you. Charts are on pages 75-78.

Celebration

A wedding calls for a truly special gift! With these romantic designs in cross stitch, you can fashion a keepsake the happy couple will cherish for years. Charts are on pages 79-82.

Bless the Beasts

Got a special place in your heart for the gentle creatures of the world?
These projects put your thoughts in stitches! Chart is on page 78.

PUT A (FUN) LID ON IT! *Shown on page 11. Continued on pages 37-39.*

X	DMC	¼X	B'ST	ANC.	COLOR	X	DMC	¼X	B'ST	ANC.	COLOR	X	DMC	¼X	B'ST	ANC.	COLOR
☆	blanc			2	white	◻	554			96	lt purple	★	898			360	brown
◕	309			42	vy dk pink	◈	699			923	dk green	✕	899			52	pink
■	310			403	black	6	744			301	yellow	S	911			205	emerald green
✳	321			9046	red	0	745			300	lt yellow	N	913			204	lt emerald green
R	335			38	dk pink	∾	754			1012	lt peach	H	3326			36	lt pink
⊙	353			6	peach	◆	798			131	dk blue	•	309			42	vy dk pink Fr. Knot
4	436			1045	tan	+	799			136	blue	•	699			923	dk green Fr. Knot
C	552			99	purple	◇	800			144	lt blue	●	798			131	dk blue Fr. Knot

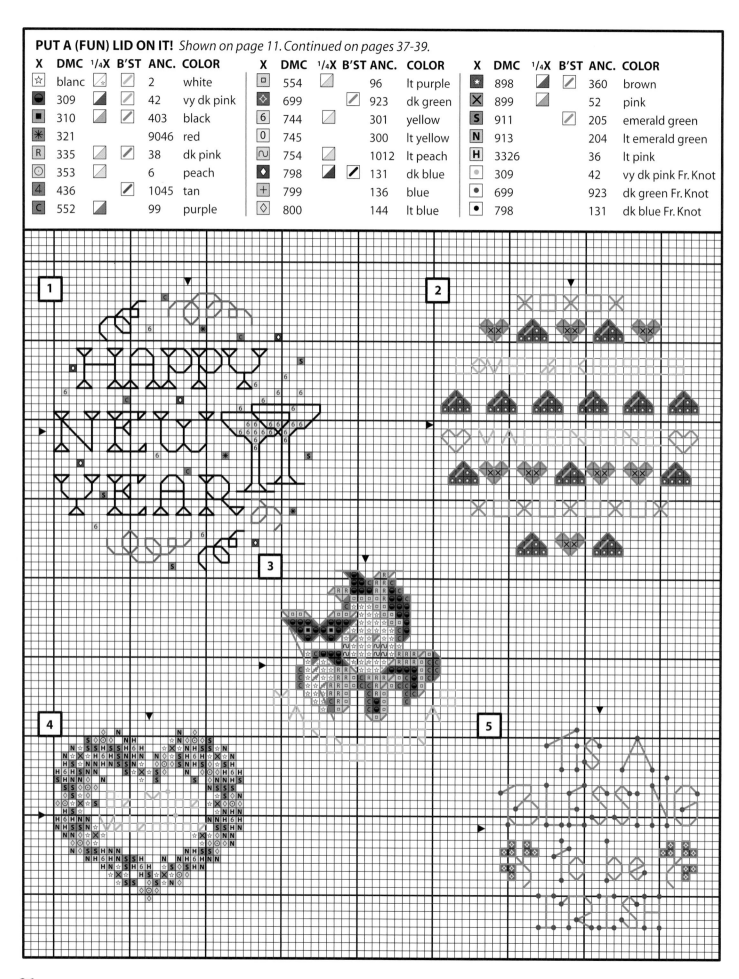

36

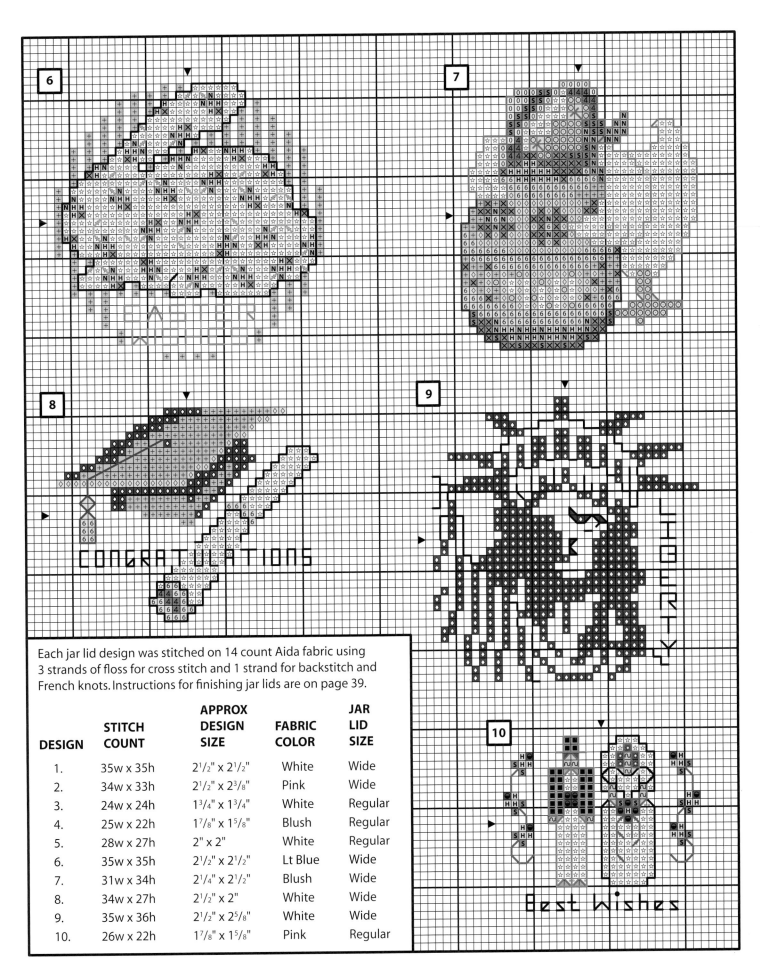

Each jar lid design was stitched on 14 count Aida fabric using 3 strands of floss for cross stitch and 1 strand for backstitch and French knots. Instructions for finishing jar lids are on page 39.

DESIGN	STITCH COUNT	APPROX DESIGN SIZE	FABRIC COLOR	JAR LID SIZE
1.	35w x 35h	$2^{1}/_{2}$" x $2^{1}/_{2}$"	White	Wide
2.	34w x 33h	$2^{1}/_{2}$" x $2^{3}/_{8}$"	Pink	Wide
3.	24w x 24h	$1^{3}/_{4}$" x $1^{3}/_{4}$"	White	Regular
4.	25w x 22h	$1^{7}/_{8}$" x $1^{5}/_{8}$"	Blush	Regular
5.	28w x 27h	2" x 2"	White	Regular
6.	35w x 35h	$2^{1}/_{2}$" x $2^{1}/_{2}$"	Lt Blue	Wide
7.	31w x 34h	$2^{1}/_{4}$" x $2^{1}/_{2}$"	Blush	Wide
8.	34w x 27h	$2^{1}/_{2}$" x 2"	White	Wide
9.	35w x 36h	$2^{1}/_{2}$" x $2^{5}/_{8}$"	White	Wide
10.	26w x 22h	$1^{7}/_{8}$" x $1^{5}/_{8}$"	Pink	Regular

PUT A (FUN) LID ON IT! (continued) *Shown on page 11.*

X	DMC	1/4X	B'ST	ANC.	COLOR
☆	blanc			2	white
▲	304			1006	dk red
◓	309	◪	◹	42	vy dk pink
■	310	◪	◹	403	black
✳	321			9046	red
R	335		◹	38	dk pink
8	434			310	dk tan
4	436			1045	tan
A	550			102	dk purple
C	552			99	purple
▫	554	◨		96	lt purple

X	DMC	1/4X	B'ST	ANC.	COLOR
◈	699	◪	◹	923	dk green
V	701	◪		227	green
△	738			361	lt tan
–	739			387	vy lt tan
3	741		◹	304	lt orange
6	744			301	yellow
∩	754		◹	1012	lt peach
2	762			234	grey
◆	798		◹	131	dk blue
+	799		◹	136	blue

X	DMC	1/4X	B'ST	ANC.	COLOR
◇	800			144	lt blue
★	898	◪	◹	360	brown
X	899			52	pink
S	911		◹	205	emerald green
N	913			204	lt emerald green
5	948		◹	1011	vy lt peach
B	970		◹	316	orange
H	3326			36	lt pink
•	310			403	black Fr. Knot
•	798			131	dk blue Fr. Knot
•	898			360	brown Fr. Knot

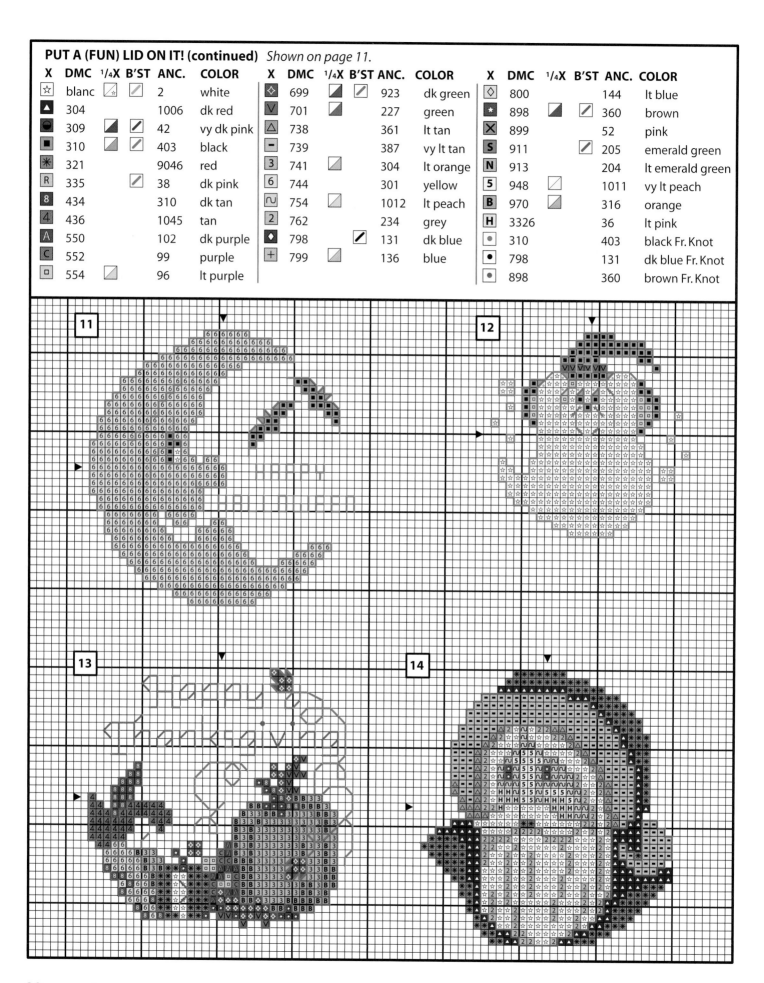

38

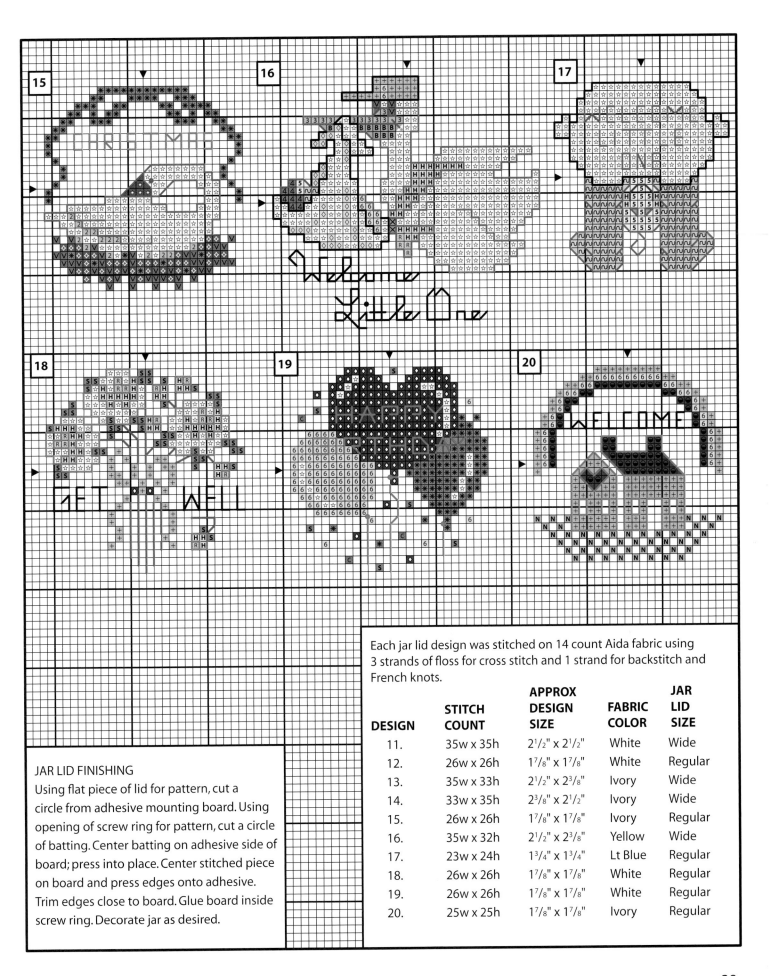

JAR LID FINISHING

Using flat piece of lid for pattern, cut a circle from adhesive mounting board. Using opening of screw ring for pattern, cut a circle of batting. Center batting on adhesive side of board; press into place. Center stitched piece on board and press edges onto adhesive. Trim edges close to board. Glue board inside screw ring. Decorate jar as desired.

Each jar lid design was stitched on 14 count Aida fabric using 3 strands of floss for cross stitch and 1 strand for backstitch and French knots.

DESIGN	STITCH COUNT	APPROX DESIGN SIZE	FABRIC COLOR	JAR LID SIZE
11.	35w x 35h	2¹/₂" x 2¹/₂"	White	Wide
12.	26w x 26h	1⁷/₈" x 1⁷/₈"	White	Regular
13.	35w x 33h	2¹/₂" x 2³/₈"	Ivory	Wide
14.	33w x 35h	2³/₈" x 2¹/₂"	Ivory	Wide
15.	26w x 26h	1⁷/₈" x 1⁷/₈"	Ivory	Regular
16.	35w x 32h	2¹/₂" x 2³/₈"	Yellow	Wide
17.	23w x 24h	1³/₄" x 1³/₄"	Lt Blue	Regular
18.	26w x 26h	1⁷/₈" x 1⁷/₈"	White	Regular
19.	26w x 26h	1⁷/₈" x 1⁷/₈"	White	Regular
20.	25w x 25h	1⁷/₈" x 1⁷/₈"	Ivory	Regular

40

HOLIDAY HOUSE (96w x 124h) *Shown on pages 12–13.* Charts continued on pages 42–43.

X	DMC	¼X	B'ST	ANC.	COLOR
∴	blanc	∷	◩	2	white
-	ecru	☐	◪	387	ecru
⊙	223			895	mauve
◇	224	◩		893	lt mauve
✲	304			1006	dk red
V	321			9046	red
✳	501			878	dk blue green
+	502			877	blue green
⊙	503			876	lt blue green
A	563			208	green
✳	640			903	dk beige

X	DMC	¼X	ANC.	COLOR
◆	642	◪	392	beige
△	644	◪	830	lt beige
○	676		891	lt gold
⊟	721		925	orange
★	722		323	lt orange
◇	726		295	yellow
✛	729		890	gold
✕	793		176	violet
△	813		161	blue
▢	822	◪	390	vy lt beige

X	DMC	B'ST	ANC.	COLOR
⊙	844		1041	dk grey
⬛	930	◩	1035	dk grey blue
V	931	◩	1034	grey blue
⊙	932		1033	lt grey blue
	3350	◩	59	dk pink
✱	3354		74	pink
▲	3371	◩	382	brown black
⊙	ecru		387	ecru Fr. Knot
●	3371		382	brown black Fr. Knot

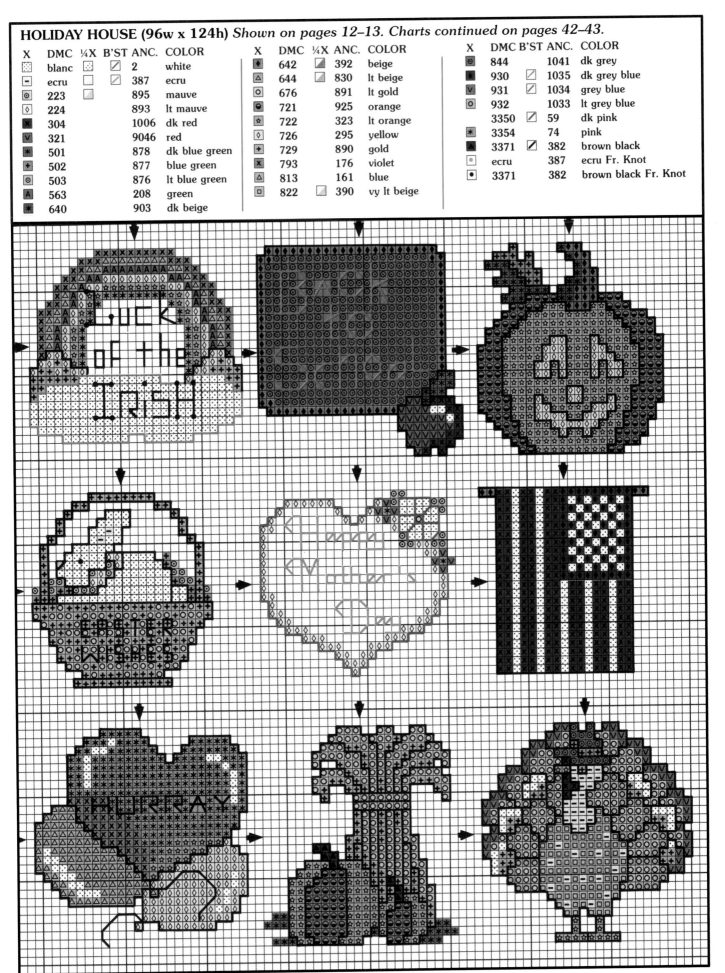

HOLIDAY HOUSE (continued)

X	DMC	B'ST	ANC.	COLOR	X	DMC	ANC.	COLOR	X	DMC	B'ST	ANC.	COLOR
	blanc	/	2	white	◆	642	392	beige	■	930	/	1035	dk grey blue
◉	223		895	mauve	△	644	830	lt beige	∨	931	/	1034	grey blue
◇	224		893	lt mauve	◎	676	891	lt gold	◎	932		1033	lt grey blue
✕	304	/	1006	dk red	✕	680	901	dk gold		3350	/	59	dk pink
∨	321		9046	red	☆	722	323	lt orange	✳	3354		74	pink
✳	501	/	878	dk blue green	✦	729	890	gold	▲	3371	/	382	brown black
✚	502		877	blue green					∘	501		878	dk blue green Fr. Knot
✹	640		903	dk beige					●	3371		382	brown black Fr. Knot

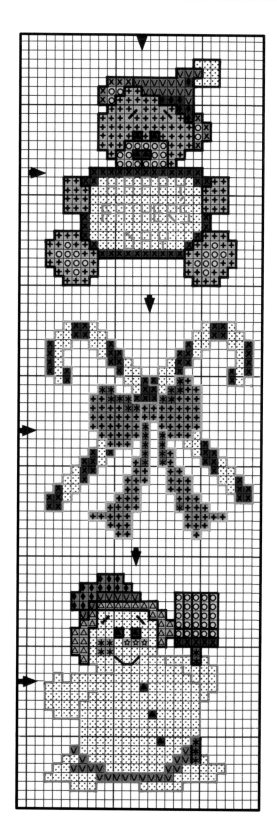

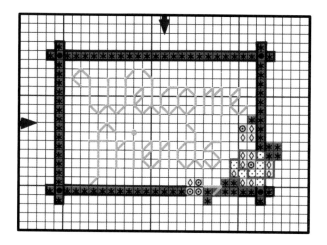

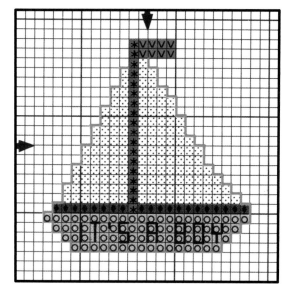

PROJECTS

Holiday House was stitched on a 13" x 14$\frac{1}{2}$" piece of Dirty Aida (14 ct) using 3 strands of floss for cross stitch, 2 strands for ecru backstitch, and 1 strand for French knots and remaining backstitch. Design size 6$\frac{7}{8}$" x 8$\frac{7}{8}$". Design was custom framed.

Door Ornaments were stitched separately on Ivory Hardanger (22 ct) using 1 strand of floss for cross stitch, 2 strands for white backstitch, and 1 strand for remaining backstitch. Design size 1$\frac{1}{8}$" x 1$\frac{1}{8}$" each. See Door Ornament Finishing, page 43.

DOOR ORNAMENT FINISHING

For each ornament, cut a piece of cotton fabric for backing the same size as stitched piece. Apply fabric stiffener to back of stitched piece. Matching wrong sides, place stitched piece on backing fabric; allow to dry. Apply stiffener to back of ornament and allow to dry; repeat for front. Cutting close to edges of design, cut out ornament.

Center and glue back of "looped" side of a ½" diameter hook and loop self-gripping fastener to back of ornament. Refer to photo to center and sew back of "hooked" side of a ½" dia. hook and loop self-gripping fastener to door of house. To attach ornament to house, press back of ornament to door, matching hook and loop fasteners.

HOLIDAY HOUSE (continued)

X	DMC	¼X	B'ST	ANC.	COLOR
⊡	blanc			2	white
⊙	223			895	mauve
◇	224			893	lt mauve
	501		▨	878	dk blue green
✦	502			877	blue green
⊙	503	◪		876	lt blue green
A	563			208	green
○	676			891	lt gold
☆	722	◪	▨	323	lt orange
◇	726	◪		295	yellow
✕	813			161	blue
	931		▨	1034	grey blue
	3350		▨	59	dk pink
✲	3354			74	pink
	3371		▨	382	brown black
●	3350			59	dk pink Fr. Knot

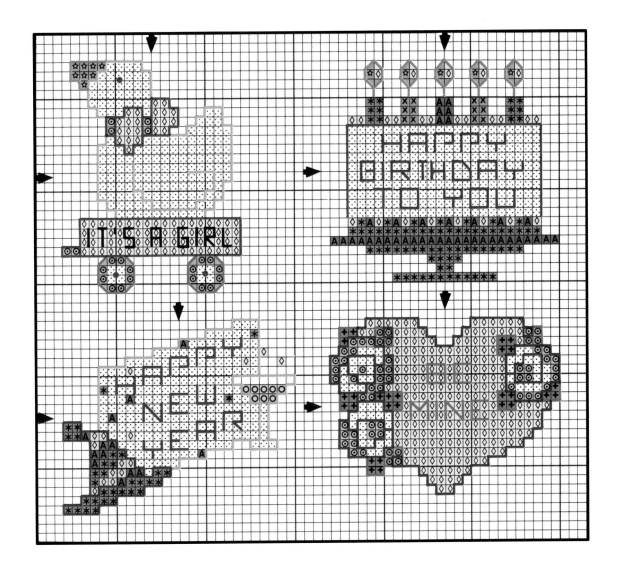

AT YOUR FINGERTIPS *Shown on pages 14-15. Charts continued on pages 46-47.*

X	DMC	¼X	B'ST	ANC.	COLOR
☆	blanc			2	white
◆	304			1006	dk red
6	309			42	dk pink
■	310			403	black
◗	318			399	dk grey
◖	334			977	blue
A	349			13	lt red
◆	415			398	grey
R	433			358	dk tan
N	435			1046	tan
5	472			253	vy lt green
★	550			102	dk purple
∿	552			99	purple

X	DMC	¼X	B'ST	ANC.	COLOR
S	554			96	lt purple
B	699			923	vy dk green
X	701			227	dk green
8	703			238	green
☆	704			256	lt green
2	721			925	lt orange
+	725			305	dk yellow
▬	726			295	yellow
○	727			293	lt yellow
◉	754			1012	peach
3	775			128	lt blue
◇	776			24	lt pink
▲	797			132	dk blue

X	DMC	¼X	B'ST	ANC.	COLOR
E	801			359	brown
✳	817			13	red
V	899			52	pink
◆	900			333	dk orange
4	947			330	orange
▢	963			73	vy lt pink
C	970			316	vy lt orange
●	blanc			2	white Fr. Knot
●	309			42	dk pink Fr. Knot
●	310			403	black Fr. Knot
●	699			923	vy dk green Fr. Knot
●	725			305	dk yellow Fr. Knot

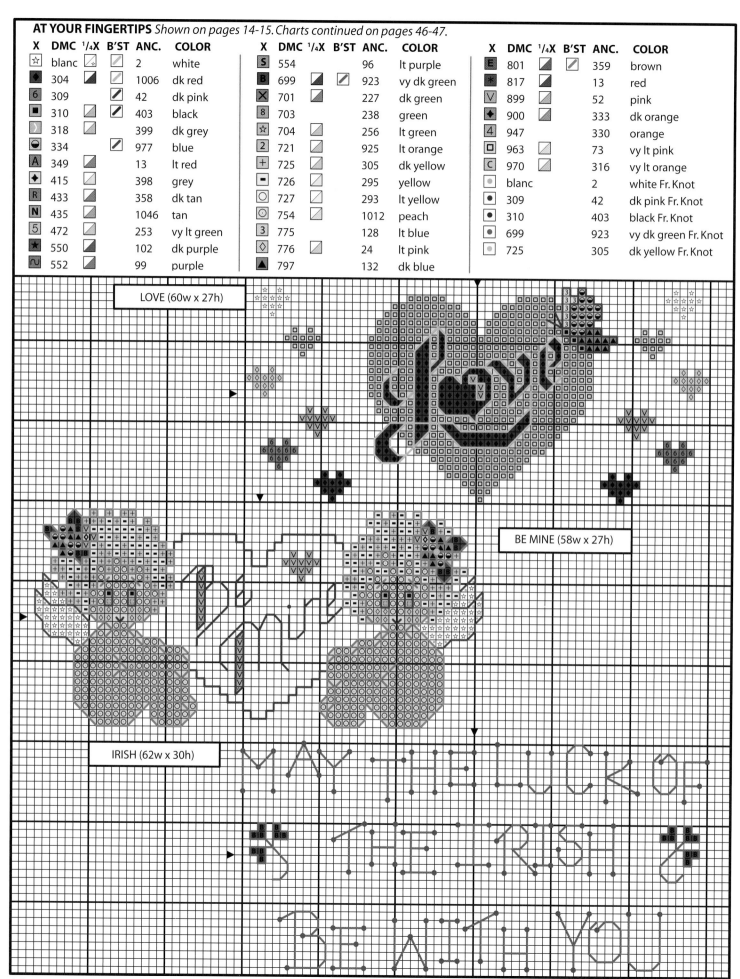

LOVE (60w x 27h)

BE MINE (58w x 27h)

IRISH (62w x 30h)

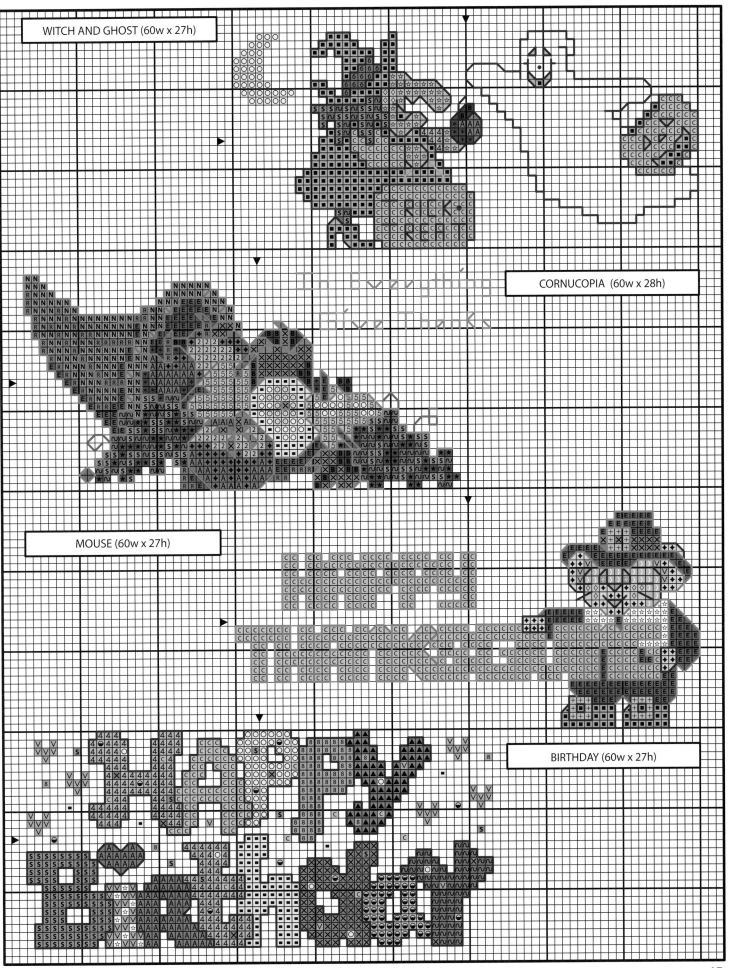

WITCH AND GHOST (60w x 27h)

CORNUCOPIA (60w x 28h)

MOUSE (60w x 27h)

BIRTHDAY (60w x 27h)

X	DMC	¼X	B'ST	ANC.	COLOR	X	DMC	¼X	B'ST	ANC.	COLOR	X	DMC	¼X	B'ST	ANC.	COLOR
☆	blanc	☆		2	white	8	703			238	green	✳	817			13	red
◆	304			1006	dk red	+	725	◪		305	dk yellow	V	899			52	pink
■	310			403	black	-	726			295	yellow	4	947			330	orange
	334			977	blue	○	727			293	lt yellow	▢	963			73	vy lt pink
A	349	◪		13	lt red	△	729	◪		890	gold	C	970	◪		316	vy lt orange
R	433	◪		358	dk tan	3	775			128	lt blue	•	blanc			2	white Fr. Knot
N	435	◪		1046	tan	◇	776			24	lt pink	•	310			403	black Fr. Knot
B	699			923	vy dk green	▲	797	◪		132	dk blue	•	701			227	dk green Fr. Knot
X	701			227	dk green	E	801			359	brown	•	817			13	red Fr. Knot

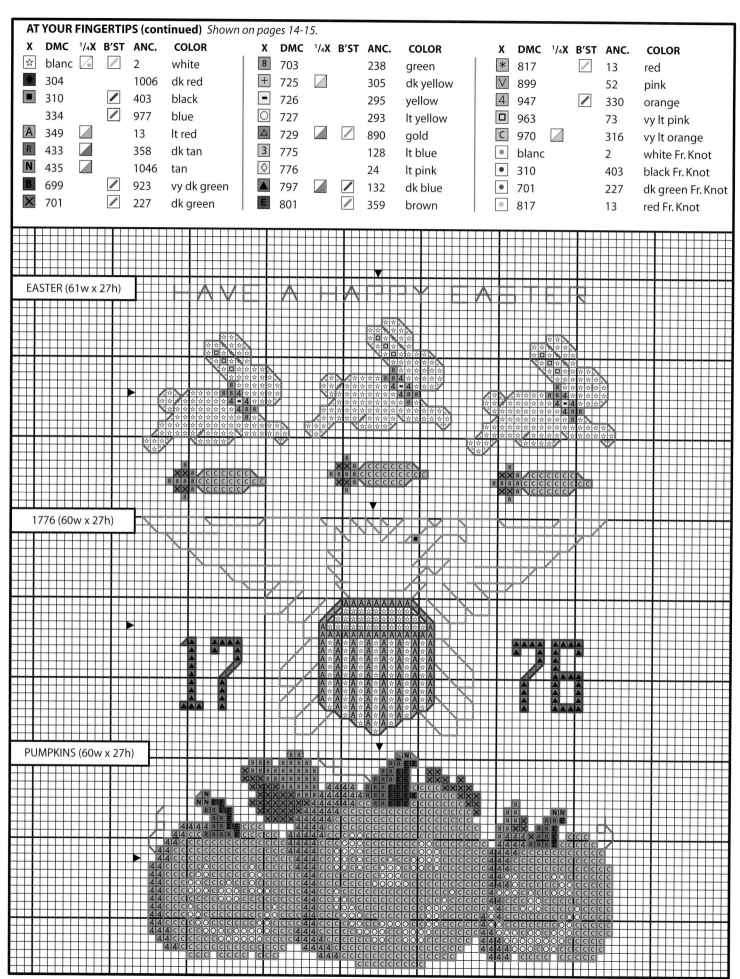

EASTER (61w x 27h)

1776 (60w x 27h)

PUMPKINS (60w x 27h)

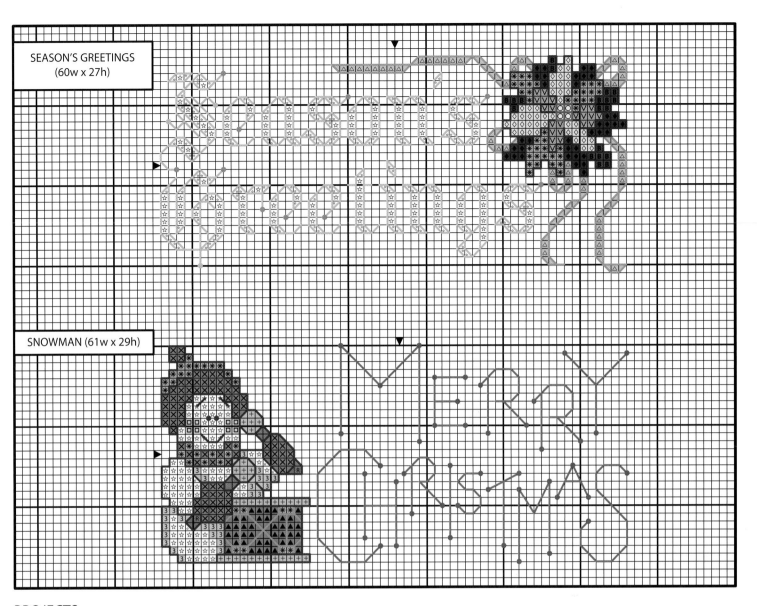

PROJECTS

Each of the designs on pages 44–47 was stitched on a prefinished hand towel with a 14 count insert using 3 strands of floss for cross stitch, 2 strands for backstitched letters (including French knots), and 1 strand for remaining backstitch and French knots.

Design	Color of Towel	Design Size
Be Mine	Light Rose	$4^1/_4$" x 2"
Birthday	White	$4^3/_8$" x 2"
Cornucopia	Parchment	$4^3/_8$" x 2"
Easter	Peach	$4^3/_8$" x 2"
Irish	White	$4^1/_2$" x $2^1/_4$"
Love	Blue Ridge	$4^3/_8$" x 2"
Mouse	Parchment	$4^3/_8$" x 2"
Pumpkins	Yellow	$4^3/_8$" x 2"
Season's Greetings	Green	$4^3/_8$" x 2"
Snowman	Red	$4^3/_8$" x $2^1/_8$"
Witch and Ghost	White	$4^3/_8$" x 2"
1776	White	$4^3/_8$" x 2"

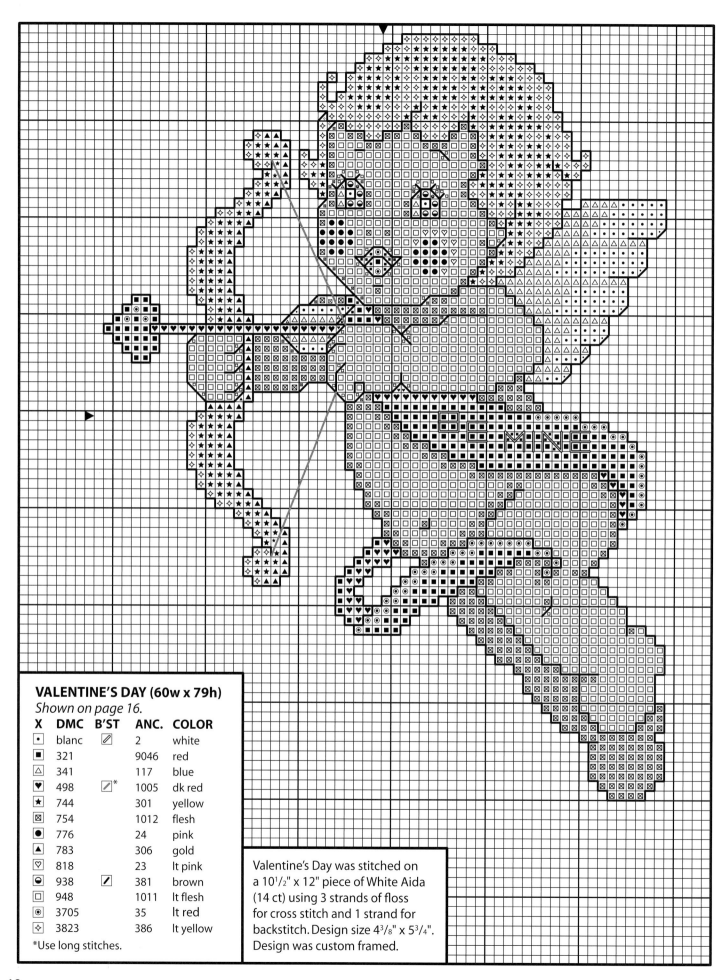

VALENTINE'S DAY (60w x 79h)
Shown on page 16.

X	DMC	B'ST	ANC.	COLOR
•	blanc	✐	2	white
■	321		9046	red
△	341		117	blue
♥	498	✐*	1005	dk red
★	744		301	yellow
⊠	754		1012	flesh
●	776		24	pink
▲	783		306	gold
♡	818		23	lt pink
◉	938	✐	381	brown
□	948		1011	lt flesh
◉	3705		35	lt red
◇	3823		386	lt yellow

*Use long stitches.

Valentine's Day was stitched on a 10¹/₂" x 12" piece of White Aida (14 ct) using 3 strands of floss for cross stitch and 1 strand for backstitch. Design size 4³/₈" x 5³/₄". Design was custom framed.

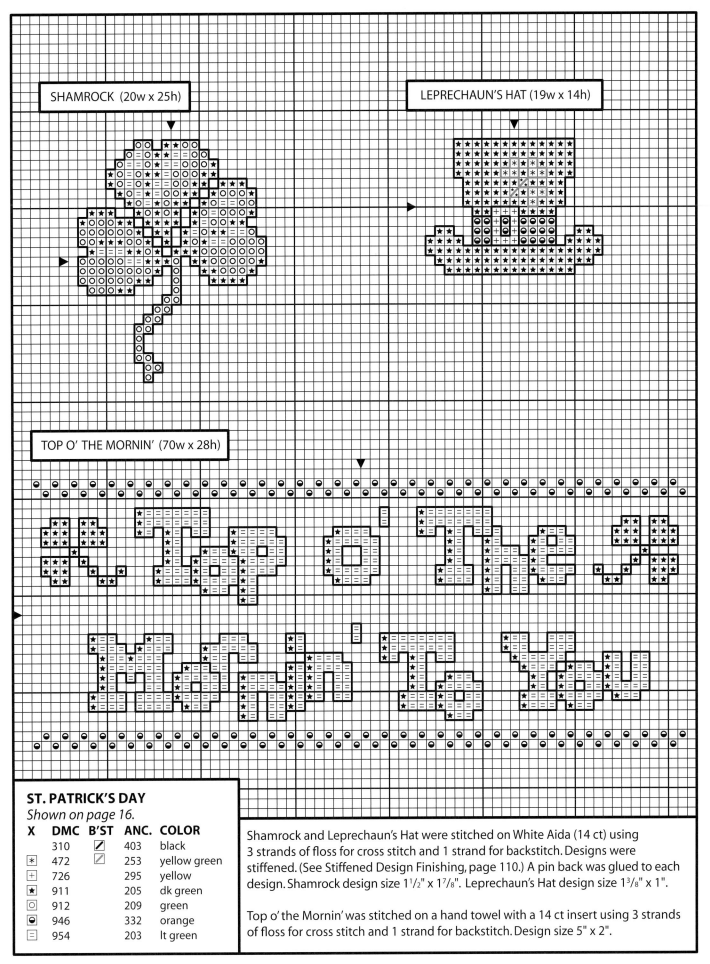

SHAMROCK (20w x 25h)

LEPRECHAUN'S HAT (19w x 14h)

TOP O' THE MORNIN' (70w x 28h)

ST. PATRICK'S DAY

Shown on page 16.

X	DMC	B'ST	ANC.	COLOR
	310	⁄	403	black
*	472	⁄	253	yellow green
+	726		295	yellow
★	911		205	dk green
○	912		209	green
◉	946		332	orange
=	954		203	lt green

Shamrock and Leprechaun's Hat were stitched on White Aida (14 ct) using 3 strands of floss for cross stitch and 1 strand for backstitch. Designs were stiffened. (See Stiffened Design Finishing, page 110.) A pin back was glued to each design. Shamrock design size 1 1/2" x 1 7/8". Leprechaun's Hat design size 1 3/8" x 1".

Top o' the Mornin' was stitched on a hand towel with a 14 ct insert using 3 strands of floss for cross stitch and 1 strand for backstitch. Design size 5" x 2".

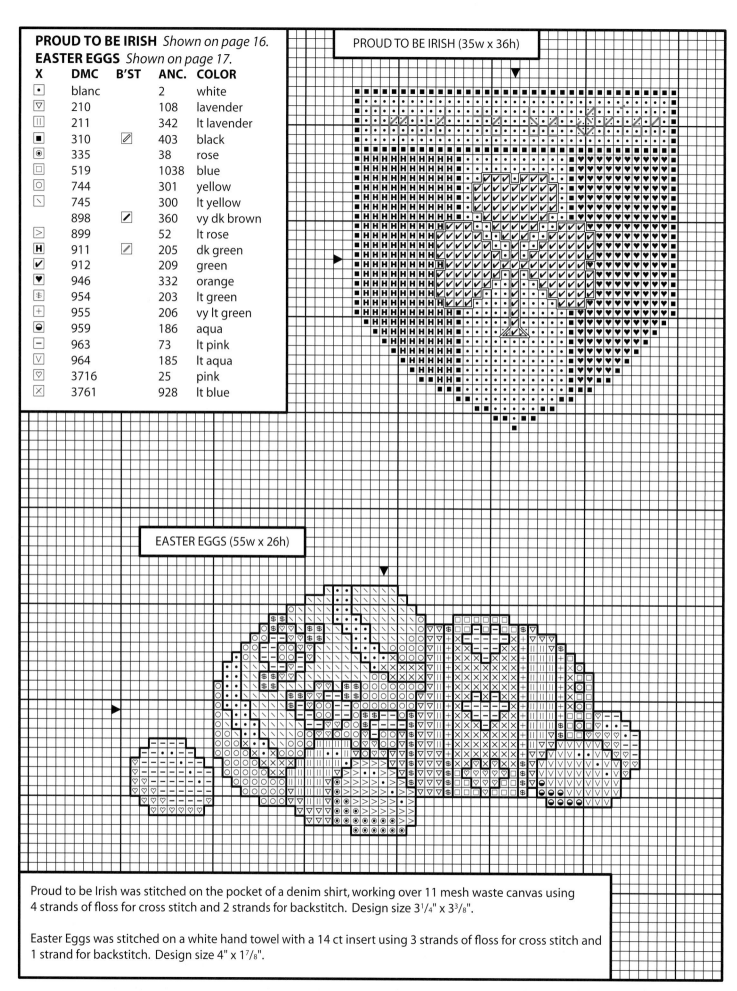

PROUD TO BE IRISH *Shown on page 16.*
EASTER EGGS *Shown on page 17.*

X	DMC	B'ST	ANC.	COLOR
·	blanc		2	white
▽	210		108	lavender
‖	211		342	lt lavender
■	310	✎	403	black
◉	335		38	rose
□	519		1038	blue
○	744		301	yellow
\	745		300	lt yellow
	898	✎	360	vy dk brown
>	899		52	lt rose
H	911	✎	205	dk green
✔	912		209	green
♥	946		332	orange
$	954		203	lt green
+	955		206	vy lt green
◐	959		186	aqua
−	963		73	lt pink
∨	964		185	lt aqua
♡	3716		25	pink
✕	3761		928	lt blue

PROUD TO BE IRISH (35w x 36h)

EASTER EGGS (55w x 26h)

Proud to be Irish was stitched on the pocket of a denim shirt, working over 11 mesh waste canvas using 4 strands of floss for cross stitch and 2 strands for backstitch. Design size 3¼" x 3⅜".

Easter Eggs was stitched on a white hand towel with a 14 ct insert using 3 strands of floss for cross stitch and 1 strand for backstitch. Design size 4" x 1⅞".

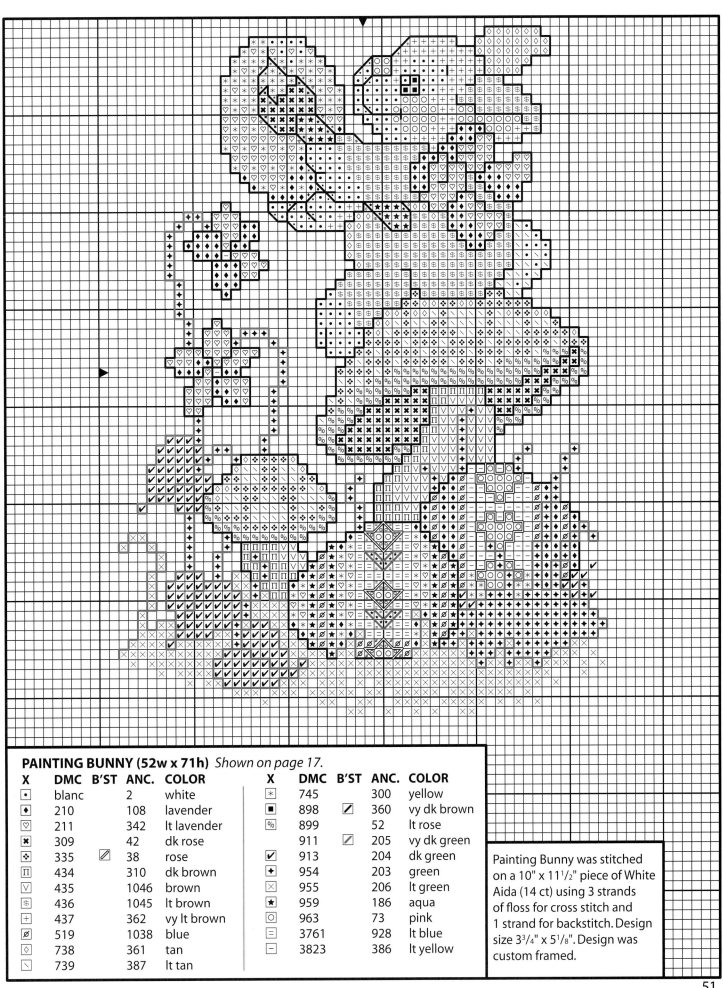

PAINTING BUNNY (52w x 71h) *Shown on page 17.*

X	DMC	B'ST	ANC.	COLOR		X	DMC	B'ST	ANC.	COLOR
•	blanc		2	white		✳	745		300	yellow
◆	210		108	lavender		■	898	✎	360	vy dk brown
♡	211		342	lt lavender		%	899		52	lt rose
✖	309		42	dk rose			911	✎	205	vy dk green
❖	335	✎	38	rose		✔	913		204	dk green
Π	434		310	dk brown		✦	954		203	green
V	435		1046	brown		✕	955		206	lt green
$	436		1045	lt brown		★	959		186	aqua
+	437		362	vy lt brown		○	963		73	pink
∅	519		1038	blue		=	3761		928	lt blue
◇	738		361	tan		−	3823		386	lt yellow
\	739		387	lt tan						

Painting Bunny was stitched on a 10" x 11½" piece of White Aida (14 ct) using 3 strands of floss for cross stitch and 1 strand for backstitch. Design size 3¾" x 5⅛". Design was custom framed.

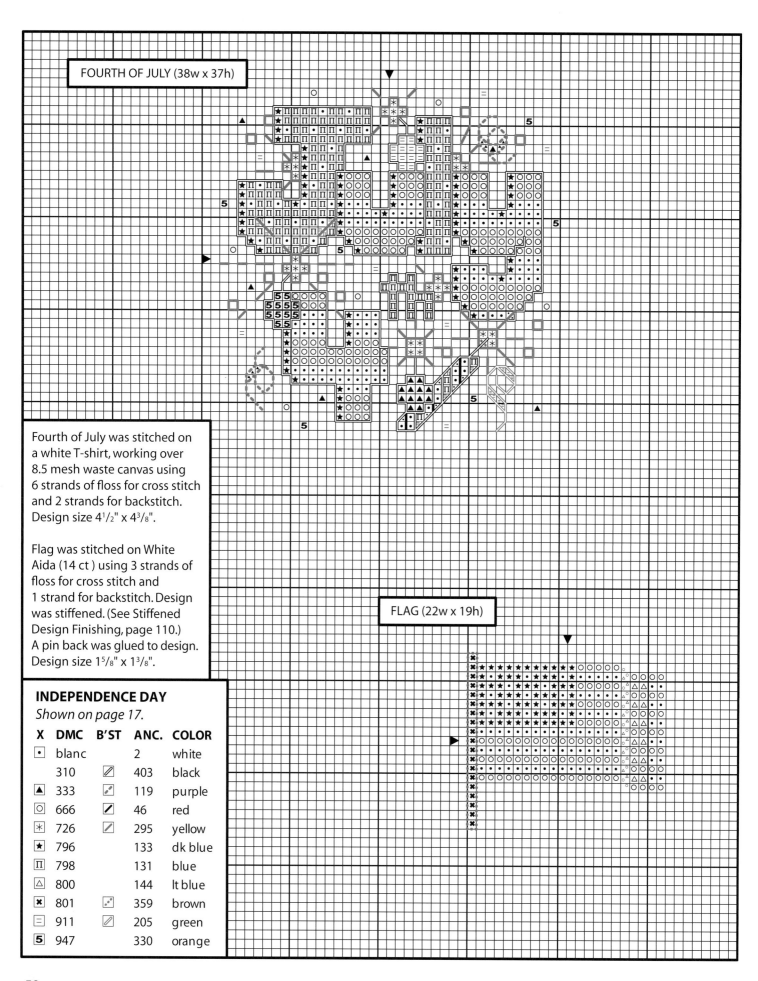

FOURTH OF JULY (38w x 37h)

Fourth of July was stitched on a white T-shirt, working over 8.5 mesh waste canvas using 6 strands of floss for cross stitch and 2 strands for backstitch. Design size 4½" x 4⅜".

Flag was stitched on White Aida (14 ct) using 3 strands of floss for cross stitch and 1 strand for backstitch. Design was stiffened. (See Stiffened Design Finishing, page 110.) A pin back was glued to design. Design size 1⅝" x 1⅜".

FLAG (22w x 19h)

INDEPENDENCE DAY
Shown on page 17.

X	DMC	B'ST	ANC.	COLOR
•	blanc		2	white
	310	✎	403	black
▲	333	✎	119	purple
○	666	✎	46	red
✳	726	✎	295	yellow
★	796		133	dk blue
∏	798		131	blue
△	800		144	lt blue
✖	801	✎	359	brown
=	911	✎	205	green
5	947		330	orange

Happy Halloween *(shown on page 18)* was stitched over 2 fabric threads on an 18" x 18" piece of Black Aida (14 ct) using 8 strands of floss for cross stitch and 3 strands for backstitch. Design size $11^5/_8$" x $11^3/_8$". Follow Wall Hanging Finishing, page 111, to make wall hanging.

Words, pumpkins, and 2 ghosts *(shown on page 3)* were stitched over 8.5 mesh waste canvas on a black sweatshirt using 6 strands of floss for cross stitch and 2 strands for backstitch. Design size $9^5/_8$" x $5^3/_8$".

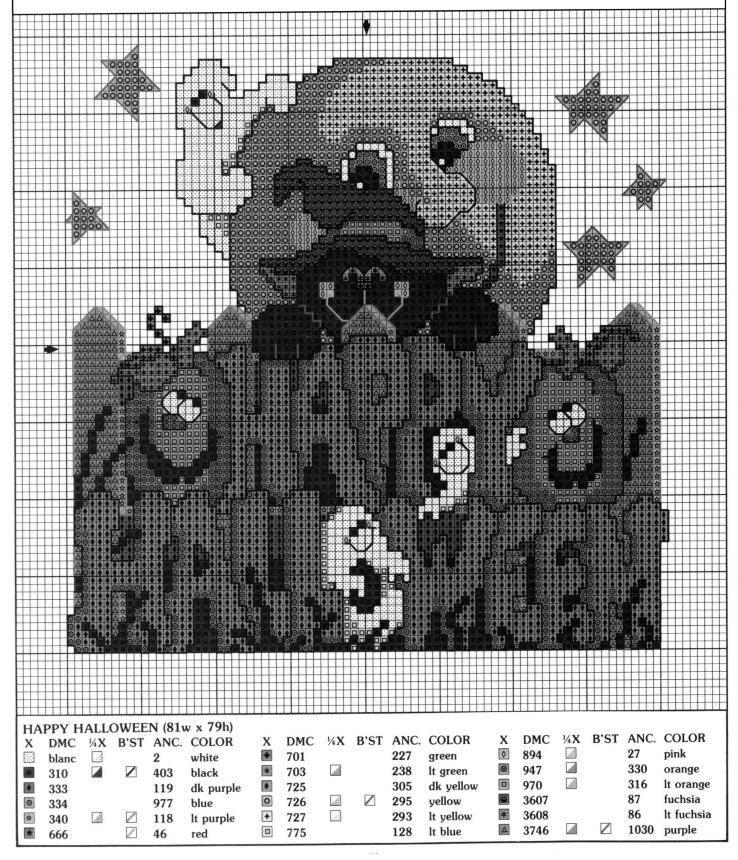

HAPPY HALLOWEEN (81w x 79h)

X	DMC	¼X	B'ST	ANC.	COLOR	X	DMC	¼X	B'ST	ANC.	COLOR	X	DMC	¼X	B'ST	ANC.	COLOR
	blanc			2	white		701			227	green		894			27	pink
	310			403	black		703			238	lt green		947			330	orange
	333			119	dk purple		725			305	dk yellow		970			316	lt orange
	334			977	blue		726			295	yellow		3607			87	fuchsia
	340			118	lt purple		727			293	lt yellow		3608			86	lt fuchsia
	666			46	red		775			128	lt blue		3746			1030	purple

Small Candy Corn **(shown on page 19)** was stitched on a Bread Cloth (14 ct) using 3 strands of floss for cross stitch and 1 strand for backstitch. Refer to photo to stitch design twice on one corner of bread cloth with outer edge of each design ³/₄" from outer edge of fringe. Stitch repeats as desired. Extend border to meet at corner of bread cloth.

Three Pumpkins **(shown on page 19)** was stitched on a white hand towel with an Aida (14 ct) insert using 3 strands of floss for cross stitch and 1 strand for backstitch. Design size 4³/₈" x 2".

Design **(shown on page 3)** was stitched over 8.5 mesh waste canvas on a purple sweatshirt using 6 strands of floss for cross stitch and 2 strands for backstitch. Design size 7¹/₈" x 3¹/₄".

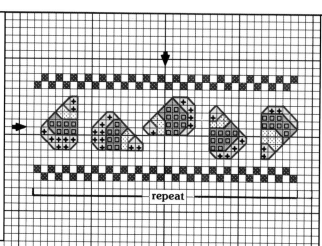

Large Candy Corn was stitched on a white hand towel with a 14 ct insert using 3 strands of floss for cross stitch and 1 strand for backstitch. Stitch repeats to edges of towel insert. For necklace and button covers, individual corn pieces were stitched over 2 fabric threads on White Hardanger (22 ct) using 4 strands of floss for cross stitch and 1 strand for backstitch. Design size 1" x 1³/₈". Follow Stiffened Design Finishing, page 110, for instructions. **Shown on pages 18–19.**

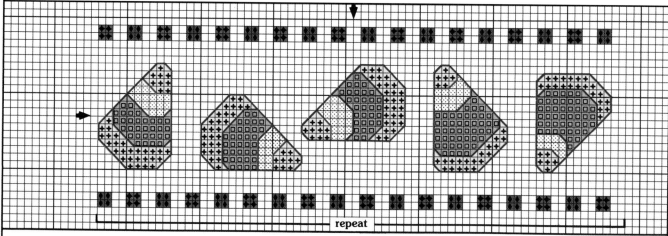

SMALL CANDY CORN (36w x 14h), WITCH (19w x 20h), SPIDER (20w x 16h), THREE PUMPKINS (60w x 27h), CAT IN WITCH HAT (27w x 24h), GHOST WITH PUMPKINS (35w x 34h), LARGE CANDY CORN (70w x 24h), CAT IN PUMPKIN (33w x 36h), BOO GHOST (31w x 39h)

X	DMC	¼X	B'ST	ANC.	COLOR	X	DMC	¼X	B'ST	ANC.	COLOR	X	DMC	¼X	ANC.	COLOR
	blanc			2	white		701			227	green		947		330	orange
	310			403	black		703			238	lt green		970		316	lt orange
	333			119	dk purple		725			305	dk yellow		3607		87	fuchsia
	334			977	blue		726			295	yellow		3608		86	lt fuchsia
	340			118	lt purple		775			128	lt blue		3746		1030	purple
	434			310	brown		894			27	pink					
	666			46	red		946			332	dk orange					

54

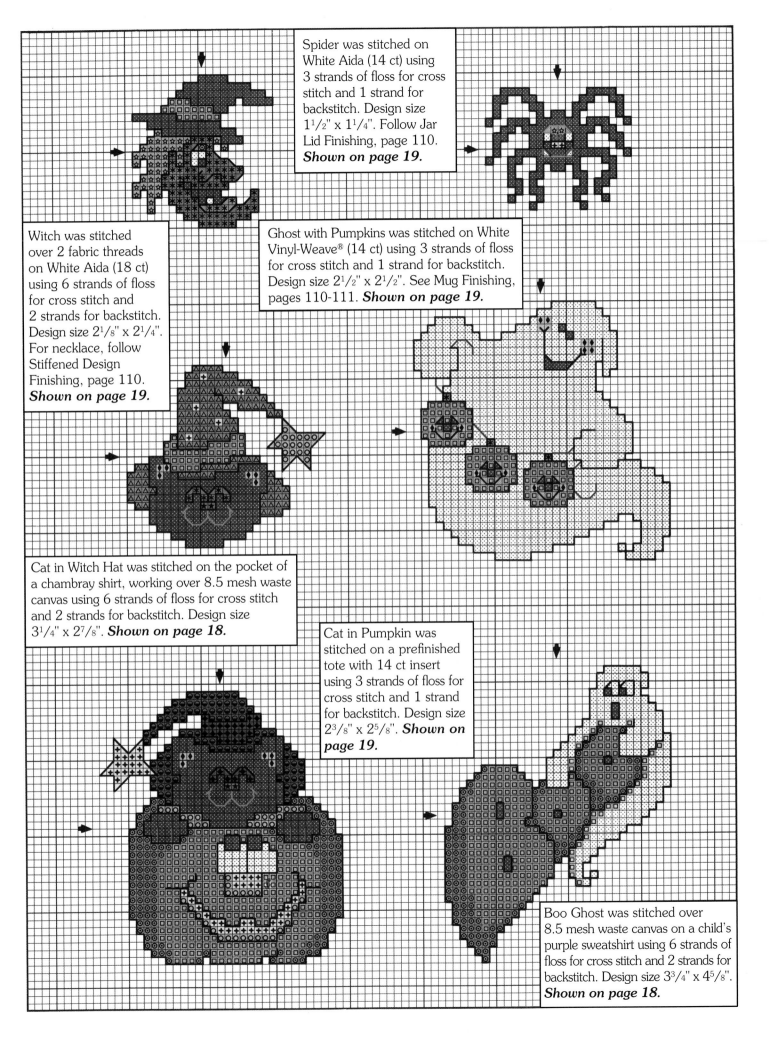

Spider was stitched on White Aida (14 ct) using 3 strands of floss for cross stitch and 1 strand for backstitch. Design size 1¹/₂" x 1¹/₄". Follow Jar Lid Finishing, page 110. *Shown on page 19.*

Witch was stitched over 2 fabric threads on White Aida (18 ct) using 6 strands of floss for cross stitch and 2 strands for backstitch. Design size 2¹/₈" x 2¹/₄". For necklace, follow Stiffened Design Finishing, page 110. *Shown on page 19.*

Ghost with Pumpkins was stitched on White Vinyl-Weave® (14 ct) using 3 strands of floss for cross stitch and 1 strand for backstitch. Design size 2¹/₂" x 2¹/₂". See Mug Finishing, pages 110-111. *Shown on page 19.*

Cat in Witch Hat was stitched on the pocket of a chambray shirt, working over 8.5 mesh waste canvas using 6 strands of floss for cross stitch and 2 strands for backstitch. Design size 3¹/₄" x 2⁷/₈". *Shown on page 18.*

Cat in Pumpkin was stitched on a prefinished tote with 14 ct insert using 3 strands of floss for cross stitch and 1 strand for backstitch. Design size 2³/₈" x 2⁵/₈". *Shown on page 19.*

Boo Ghost was stitched over 8.5 mesh waste canvas on a child's purple sweatshirt using 6 strands of floss for cross stitch and 2 strands for backstitch. Design size 3³/₄" x 4⁵/₈". *Shown on page 18.*

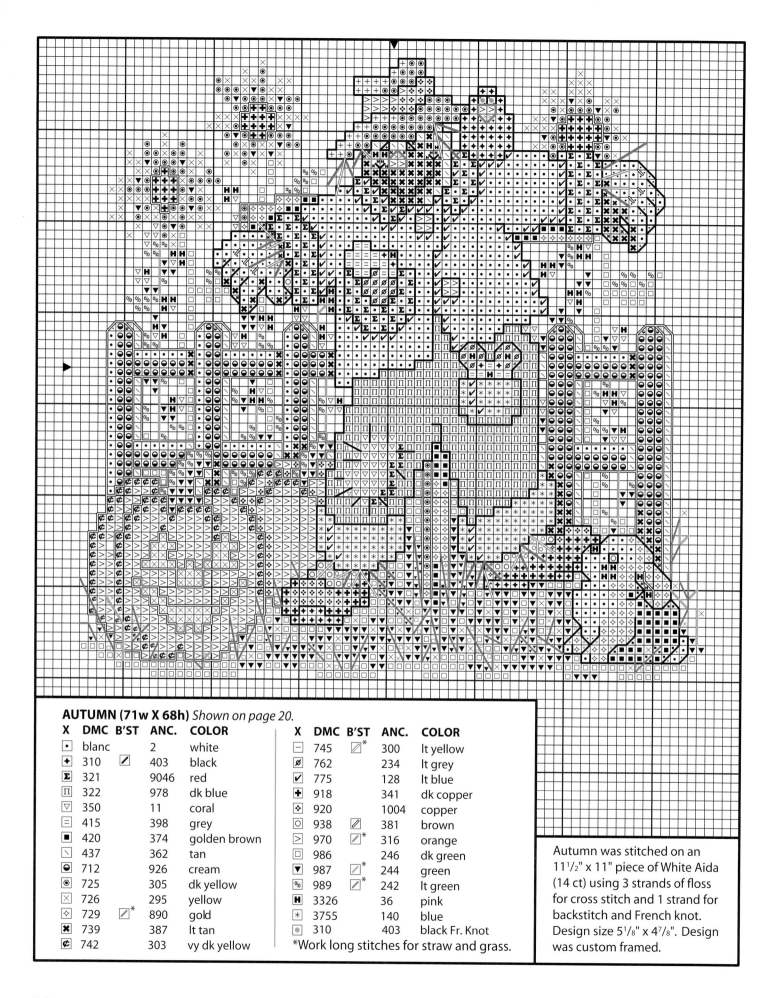

AUTUMN (71w X 68h) *Shown on page 20.*

X	DMC	B'ST	ANC.	COLOR
•	blanc		2	white
✦	310	◿	403	black
Σ	321		9046	red
Π	322		978	dk blue
▽	350		11	coral
=	415		398	grey
■	420		374	golden brown
\	437		362	tan
◒	712		926	cream
◉	725		305	dk yellow
✕	726		295	yellow
✧	729	◿*	890	gold
✖	739		387	lt tan
¢	742		303	vy dk yellow

X	DMC	B'ST	ANC.	COLOR
−	745	◿*	300	lt yellow
∅	762		234	lt grey
✔	775		128	lt blue
✚	918		341	dk copper
✦	920		1004	copper
○	938	◿	381	brown
>	970	◿*	316	orange
□	986		246	dk green
▼	987	◿*	244	green
%	989	◿*	242	lt green
H	3326		36	pink
✳	3755		140	blue
⊙	310		403	black Fr. Knot

*Work long stitches for straw and grass.

Autumn was stitched on an 11¹⁄₂" x 11" piece of White Aida (14 ct) using 3 strands of floss for cross stitch and 1 strand for backstitch and French knot. Design size 5¹⁄₈" x 4⁷⁄₈". Design was custom framed.

1. (70w x 30h)

2. (75w x 30h)

THANKSGIVING #1 and #2 *Shown on page 20.*

X	DMC	B'ST	ANC.	COLOR
•	blanc		2	white
■	310	/	403	black
◈	340		118	periwinkle
E	720		326	burnt orange
✕	726		295	yellow
2	729		890	gold
□	772		259	lt green

X	DMC	B'ST	ANC.	COLOR
▷	818		23	pink
◆	838	/	1088	brown
\	970		316	orange
★	975		355	rust
✳	977		1002	lt rust
H	987	/	244	dk green
⊙	989		242	green

Thanksgiving #1 (design size 5" x 2¼") and #2 (design size 5³⁄₈" x 2¼") were stitched on white hand towels with 14 ct inserts using 3 strands of floss for cross stitch and 1 strand for backstitch.

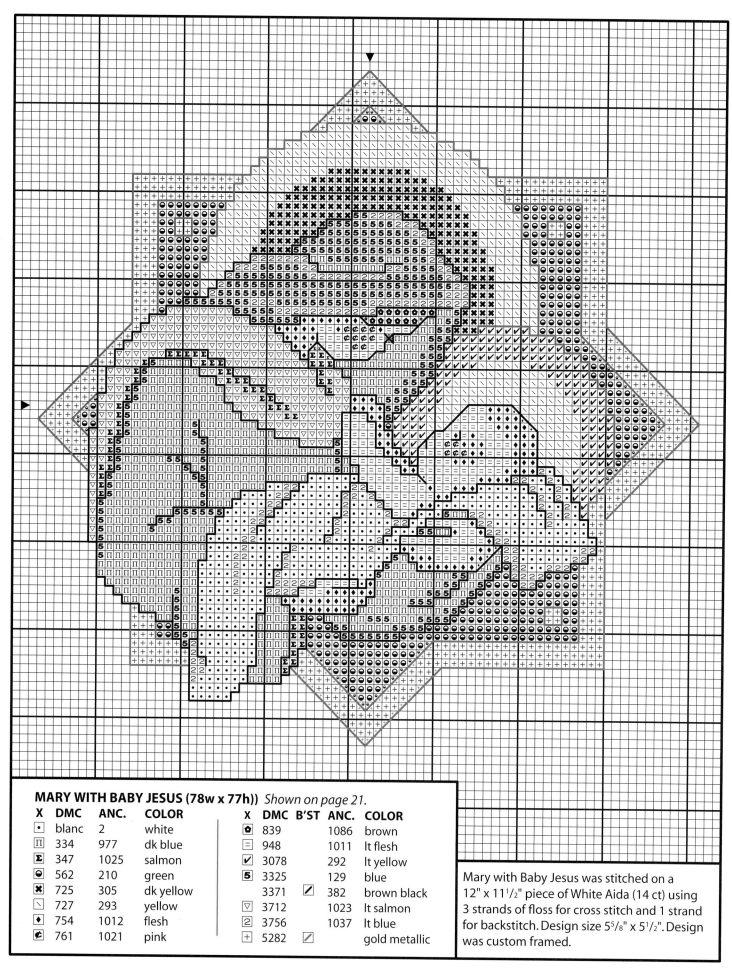

MARY WITH BABY JESUS (78w x 77h)) *Shown on page 21.*

X	DMC	ANC.	COLOR
·	blanc	2	white
Π	334	977	dk blue
Σ	347	1025	salmon
☺	562	210	green
✖	725	305	dk yellow
╲	727	293	yellow
◆	754	1012	flesh
ℓ	761	1021	pink

X	DMC	B'ST	ANC.	COLOR
✿	839		1086	brown
=	948		1011	lt flesh
✔	3078		292	lt yellow
5	3325		129	blue
	3371	╱	382	brown black
▽	3712		1023	lt salmon
2	3756		1037	lt blue
+	5282	╱		gold metallic

Mary with Baby Jesus was stitched on a 12" x 11½" piece of White Aida (14 ct) using 3 strands of floss for cross stitch and 1 strand for backstitch. Design size 5⅝" x 5½". Design was custom framed.

58

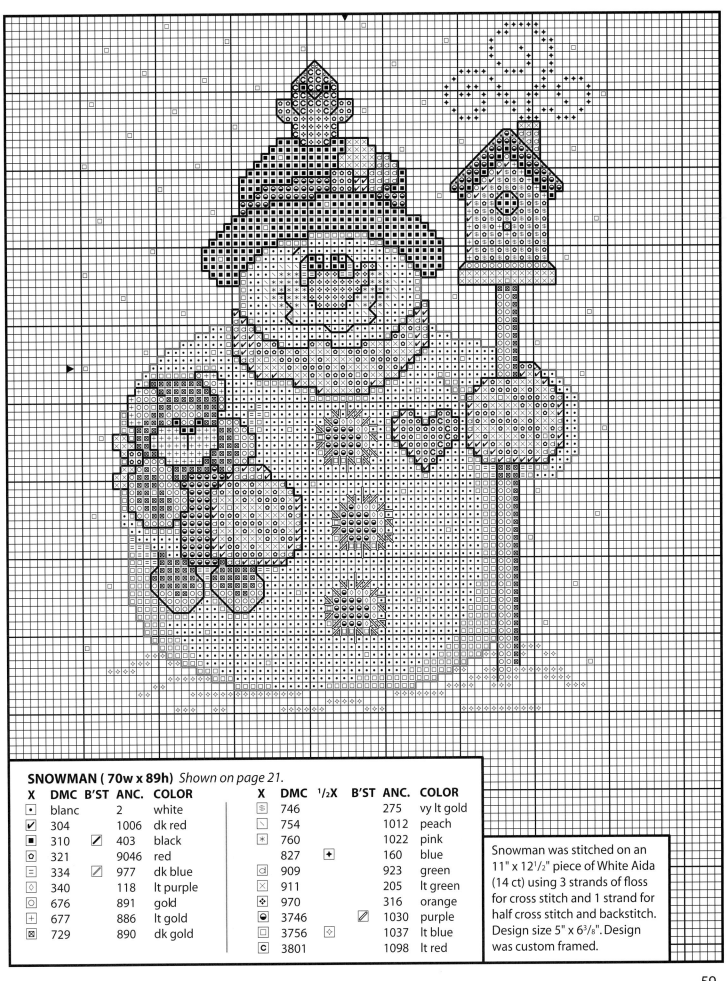

SNOWMAN (70w x 89h) *Shown on page 21.*

X	DMC	B'ST	ANC.	COLOR
•	blanc		2	white
✔	304		1006	dk red
■	310	⁄	403	black
⚙	321		9046	red
=	334	⁄	977	dk blue
◇	340		118	lt purple
○	676		891	gold
+	677		886	lt gold
⊠	729		890	dk gold

X	DMC	½X	B'ST	ANC.	COLOR
$	746			275	vy lt gold
\	754			1012	peach
*	760			1022	pink
	827		✚	160	blue
d	909			923	green
✕	911			205	lt green
❖	970			316	orange
◉	3746		⁄	1030	purple
▢	3756	◇		1037	lt blue
C	3801			1098	lt red

Snowman was stitched on an 11" x 12½" piece of White Aida (14 ct) using 3 strands of floss for cross stitch and 1 strand for half cross stitch and backstitch. Design size 5" x 6³⁄₈". Design was custom framed.

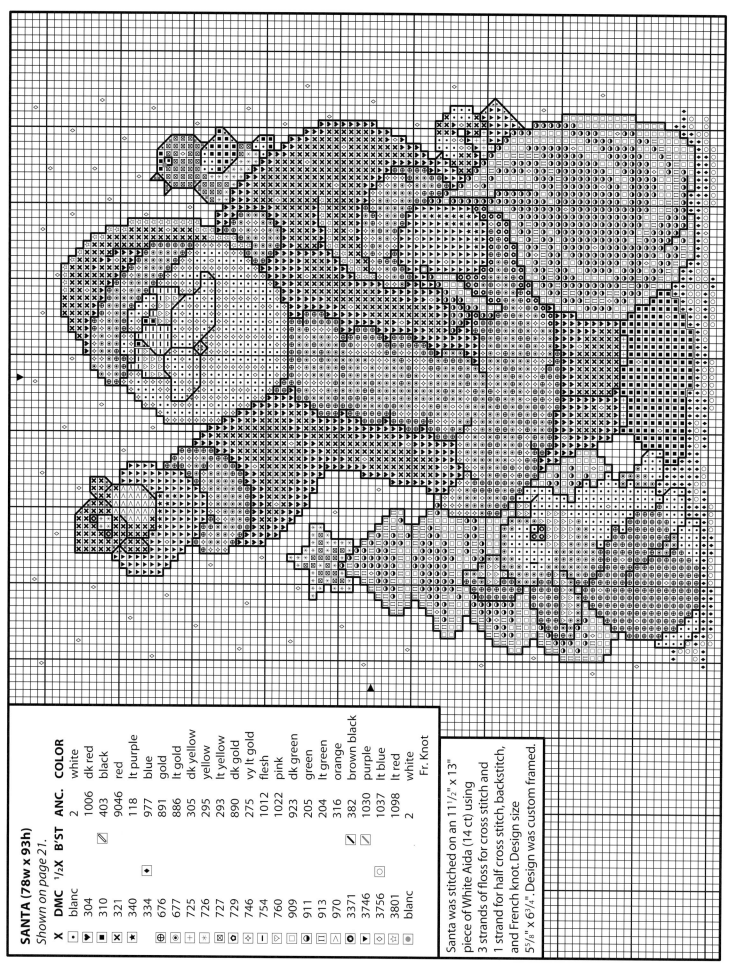

SANTA (78w x 93h)

Shown on page 21.

X	DMC	1/2X	B'ST	ANC.	COLOR
•	blanc			2	white
♥	304			1006	dk red
■	310		⁄	403	black
×	321			9046	red
★	340			118	lt purple
	334	◆		977	blue
⊕	676			891	gold
⊙	677			886	lt gold
+	725			305	dk yellow
✳	726			295	yellow
⊠	727			293	lt yellow
✿	729			890	dk gold
✧	746			275	vy lt gold
−	754			1012	flesh
♡	760			1022	pink
□	909			923	dk green
◒	911			205	green
Π	913			204	lt green
>	970			316	orange
✪	3371		⁄	382	brown black
▼	3746		⁄	1030	purple
◇	3756	○		1037	lt blue
☆	3801			1098	lt red
●	blanc			2	white Fr. Knot

Santa was stitched on an 11 1/2" x 13" piece of White Aida (14 ct) using 3 strands of floss for cross stitch and 1 strand for half cross stitch, backstitch, and French knot. Design size 5 5/8" x 6 3/4". Design was custom framed.

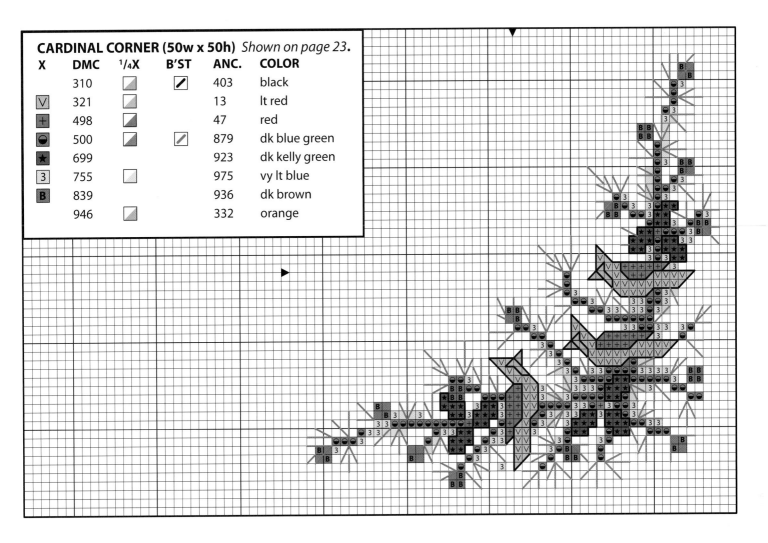

CARDINAL CORNER (50w x 50h) *Shown on page 23.*

X	DMC	¼X	B'ST	ANC.	COLOR
	310	◩	◿	403	black
V	321	◩		13	lt red
+	498	◩		47	red
⬤	500	◩	◿	879	dk blue green
★	699	◩		923	dk kelly green
3	755	◩		975	vy lt blue
B	839	◩		936	dk brown
	946	◩		332	orange

- Cardinal Corner was stitched over 2 fabric threads on Light Brown Linen (26 ct) using 3 strands of floss for cross stitch and 1 strand for backstitch. Design size 3⁷/₈" x 3⁷/₈".

For bread cloth, cut fabric 18" x 18". Machine stitch ¹/₂" from all raw edges. Stitch design with center 3¹/₂" from bottom and right edges of fabric. Unravel fabric to machine-stitched lines.

- Large Red Santa (chart on page 62) was stitched over 2 fabric threads on Cream Davosa (18 ct) using 2 strands for cross stitch and 1 strand for backstitch and French knots. Design size 6" x 9".

To make wall hanging, cut fabric to 16" x 22". After completing design, trim stitched piece to 11³/₄" x 17³/₄". Fold side edges under ¹/₂" and press; fold under ¹/₂" again and hem. For casing, fold top edge under ¹/₄" and press; fold under 1¹/₂" and hem. For fringe, machine-stitch 1" from bottom edge

and unravel fabric to machine-stitched line. Insert a purchased rod through casing or make a rod. To make a rod, cut a purchased dowel to desired length. Glue on end caps and paint or stain.

- Small Red Santa (chart on page 62) was stitched on an 8" x 9¹/₂" piece of Cream Davosa (18 ct) using 2 strands of floss for cross stitch and 1 strand for backstitch and French knots. Design size 1⁷/₈" x 3¹/₄".

To make stuffed Santa, cut stitched piece and backing fabric 2" larger than design on all sides. Matching right sides, sew fabric pieces together ¹/₄" from design, leaving an opening for turning and stuffing. Cut out Santa, leaving a ¹/₄" seam allowance. Clip curves and turn right side out. Stuff with polyester fiberfill and slipstitch opening closed.

- Blue Santa (chart on page 63) was stitched over 2 fabric threads on

Oatmeal Floba (18 ct) using 4 strands of floss for cross stitch and 2 strands for backstitch and French knots. Design size 4¹/₈" x 5³/₈".

To make a 7" x 12" bag, cut fabric 8" x 13". Center and stitch design with bottom of design 2" from one short edge. Cut backing fabric same size as stitched piece. With right sides together and using a ¹/₂" seam allowance, sew stitched piece and backing fabric together along sides and bottom. Trim corner seam allowances diagonally. Fold top edge of bag ¹/₄" to wrong side; fold under ¹/₄" again and hem. Turn right side out. Insert a piece of floral foam and flowers into bag. Referring to photo, tie braided floss around bag.

- Green Santa (chart on page 63) was stitched over 2 fabric threads on Clay Linda (27 ct) using 3 strands of floss for cross stitch and 1 strand for backstitch and French knots. Design size 2⁵/₈" x 4³/₈". Design was custom framed.

LARGE RED SANTA (54w x 80h)
SMALL RED SANTA (32w x 58h)

X	DMC	¼X	B'ST	ANC.	COLOR
▦	blanc	▦		02	white
◉	744		◪	0305	yellow
−	676	◪		0891	lt gold
2	680	◪		0901	dk gold
◈	946	◪		0332	orange
▨	948	◪		0892	flesh
▣	761	◪		08	lt pink
◉	760	◪		09	pink
V	321			013	lt red
+	498	◪	◪	047	red
▲	815	◪		043	dk red
✳	814	◪		044	vy dk red

X	DMC	¼X	B'ST	ANC.	COLOR
C	775	◪		0975	vy lt blue
★	807	◪		0168	lt blue
✳	806	◪		0169	blue
▲	312	◪	◪	0979	dk blue
3	368	◪		0214	lt green
◆	367	◪		0217	green
✕	911	◪		0205	kelly green
★	699	◪		0923	dk kelly green
◉	500			0879	dk blue green
A	842	◪		0376	vy lt brown
8	841	◪		0378	lt brown
4	840	◪		0379	brown

X	DMC	¼X	B'ST	ANC.	COLOR
B	839			0936	dk brown
■	838	◪		0381	vy dk brown
6	822	◪		0390	lt grey brown
N	644	◪	◪	0391	grey brown
E	642	◪	◪	0392	dk grey brown
H	640	◪		0393	vy dk grey brown
5	645	◪		0400	dk grey
■	310	◪	◪	0403	black
	gold		◪		metallic
□	676				lt gold Fr. Knot
●	310				black Fr. Knot
●	gold				metallic Fr. Knot

Santas are shown on pages 22–23. Instructions are on page 61.

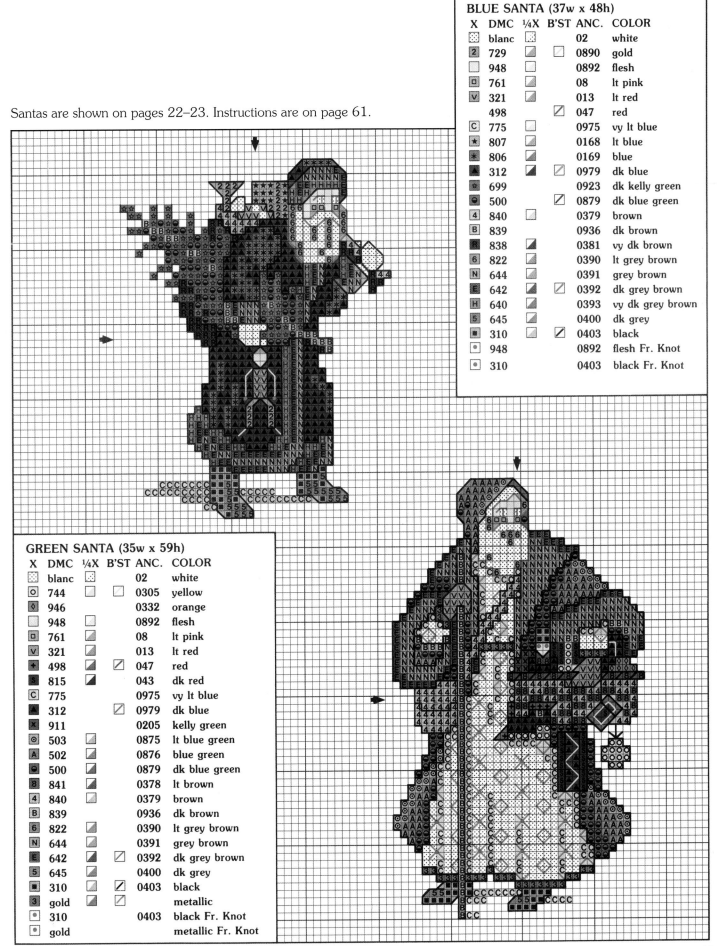

BLUE SANTA (37w x 48h)

X	DMC	¼X	B'ST	ANC.	COLOR
	blanc			02	white
2	729	◨	☐	0890	gold
	948	☐		0892	flesh
◻	761	◨		08	lt pink
V	321	◨		013	lt red
	498		◨	047	red
C	775	☐		0975	vy lt blue
★	807	◨		0168	lt blue
✳	806	◨		0169	blue
▲	312	◨	◨	0979	dk blue
✿	699			0923	dk kelly green
◉	500		◨	0879	dk blue green
4	840	☐		0379	brown
B	839			0936	dk brown
▩	838	◨		0381	vy dk brown
6	822	◨		0390	lt grey brown
N	644	◨		0391	grey brown
E	642	◨	◨	0392	dk grey brown
H	640	◨		0393	vy dk grey brown
5	645	◨		0400	dk grey
▪	310	◨	◨	0403	black
◉	948			0892	flesh Fr. Knot
◉	310			0403	black Fr. Knot

GREEN SANTA (35w x 59h)

X	DMC	¼X	B'ST	ANC.	COLOR
	blanc	▨		02	white
◉	744	☐	☐	0305	yellow
◇	946			0332	orange
	948	☐		0892	flesh
◻	761	◨		08	lt pink
V	321	◨		013	lt red
✦	498	◨	◨	047	red
▨	815	◼		043	dk red
C	775			0975	vy lt blue
▲	312		◨	0979	dk blue
✖	911			0205	kelly green
◉	503	◨		0875	lt blue green
A	502	◨		0876	blue green
◕	500	◨		0879	dk blue green
▨	841	◨		0378	lt brown
4	840	☐		0379	brown
B	839			0936	dk brown
6	822	◨		0390	lt grey brown
N	644	◨		0391	grey brown
E	642	◨	◨	0392	dk grey brown
5	645	◨		0400	dk grey
▪	310	◨	◨	0403	black
3	gold	◨	◨		metallic
◉	310			0403	black Fr. Knot
◉	gold				metallic Fr. Knot

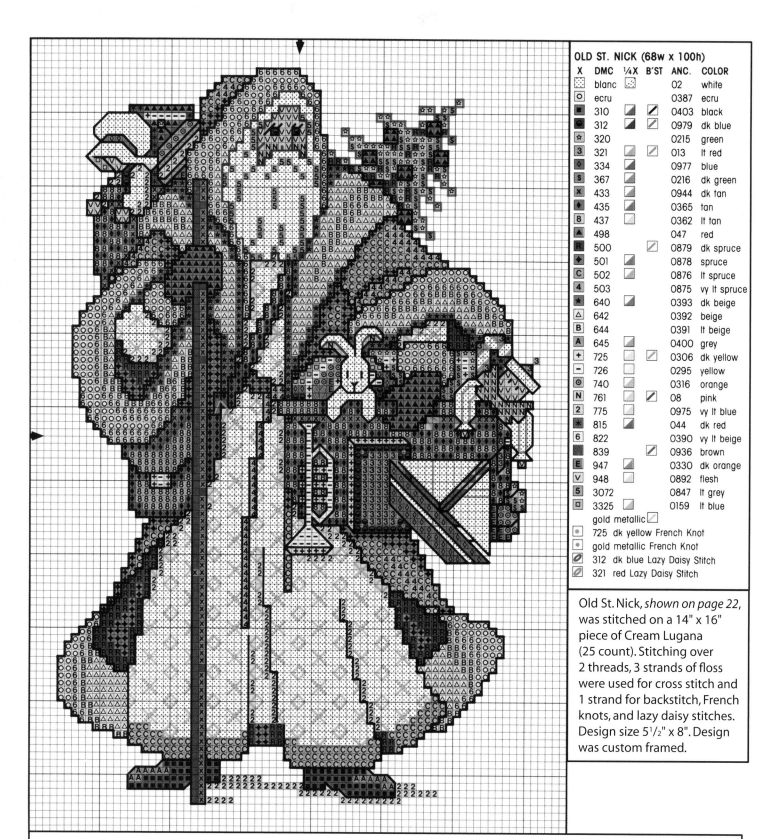

X	DMC	¼X	B'ST	ANC.	COLOR
	blanc			02	white
O	ecru			0387	ecru
	310	◢	◢	0403	black
	312	◢	◢	0979	dk blue
	320			0215	green
3	321	◢	◢	013	lt red
◇	334	◢		0977	blue
S	367	◢		0216	dk green
X	433	◢		0944	dk tan
◆	435	◢		0365	tan
8	437			0362	lt tan
▲	498			047	red
R	500		◢	0879	dk spruce
✦	501	◢		0878	spruce
C	502	◢		0876	lt spruce
4	503			0875	vy lt spruce
★	640	◢		0393	dk beige
△	642			0392	beige
B	644			0391	lt beige
A	645	◢		0400	grey
+	725		◢	0306	dk yellow
−	726			0295	yellow
⊙	740			0316	orange
N	761		◢	08	pink
2	775			0975	vy lt blue
✱	815	◢		044	dk red
6	822			0390	vy lt beige
	839		◢	0936	brown
E	947	◢		0330	dk orange
V	948			0892	flesh
S	3072			0847	lt grey
□	3325	◢		0159	lt blue
	gold metallic	◢			
⊙	725	dk yellow French Knot			
⊙	gold metallic French Knot				
◢	312	dk blue Lazy Daisy Stitch			
◢	321	red Lazy Daisy Stitch			

OLD ST. NICK (68w x 100h)

Old St. Nick, *shown on page 22,* was stitched on a 14" x 16" piece of Cream Lugana (25 count). Stitching over 2 threads, 3 strands of floss were used for cross stitch and 1 strand for backstitch, French knots, and lazy daisy stitches. Design size 5½" x 8". Design was custom framed.

Old St. Nick, *shown on page 2,* was stitched on a 1¼ yd piece of Cracked Wheat Ragusa (14 count). For afghan, cut off fabric selvages. Fabric should measure 45"w x 55"l. To make fringe, measure 5" from one edge of fabric and pull out one thread. Unravel fabric up to missing thread. Repeat for each side.

Tie an overhand knot at each corner with 4 horizontal and 4 vertical fabric threads. Working from corners, use 8 fabric threads for each knot until all threads are knotted. Folding ribbon at an angle at corners, overlapping ends of ribbon, and turning under ½" of top ribbon end, machine stitch 4 yds of ⅞"w reversible ribbon

4½" from fringe on all sides of fabric. To mark design placement, tie a piece of thread to fabric 9" from bottom ribbon and 7" from right side ribbon. Match center of design to tied thread. Stitching over 2 fabric threads, use 6 strands for cross stitch and 2 for backstitch, French knots, and lazy daisy stitches.

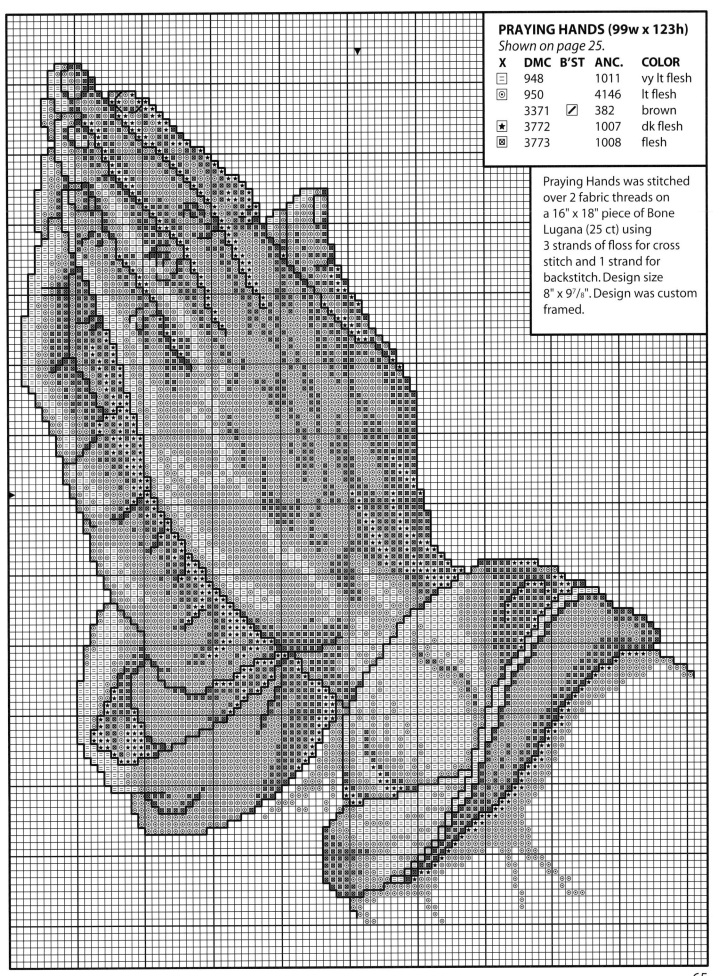

PRAYING HANDS (99w x 123h)
Shown on page 25.

X	DMC	B'ST	ANC.	COLOR
=	948		1011	vy lt flesh
⊙	950		4146	lt flesh
	3371	∕	382	brown
★	3772		1007	dk flesh
⊠	3773		1008	flesh

Praying Hands was stitched over 2 fabric threads on a 16" x 18" piece of Bone Lugana (25 ct) using 3 strands of floss for cross stitch and 1 strand for backstitch. Design size 8" x 9⁷/₈". Design was custom framed.

ORNAMENTS FOR TREE & MORE *Shown on page 24. Charts continued on pages 68–69.*

X	DMC	¼X	B'ST	ANC.	COLOR	X	DMC	¼X	B'ST	ANC.	COLOR	X	DMC	¼X	ANC.	COLOR
	blanc			2	white		699			923	dk green		920		1004	dk rust
	ecru			387	ecru		701			227	green		921		1003	rust
	310		⟋	403	black		702			226	lt green		922		1003	lt rust
	321		⟋	9046	dk red		725			305	yellow		962		75	pink
	353			6	peach		738			361	vy lt tan		3716		25	lt pink
	433			358	dk brown		754			1012	flesh		3756		1037	lt baby blue
	435			1046	brown		775			128	baby blue		3766		167	aqua
	436			1045	tan		783			306	gold					
	437			362	lt tan		797		⟋	132	blue					
	666			46	red											

28w x 33h · 34w x 32h

26w x 33h · 34w x 33h

29w x 33h

32w x 34h

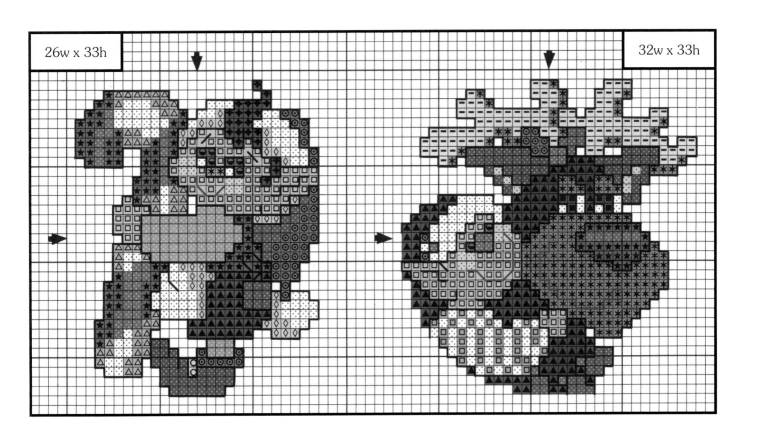

26w x 33h

32w x 33h

ORNAMENTS FOR TREE & MORE (continued) *Shown on page 24.*

X	DMC	B'ST	ANC.	COLOR	X	DMC	¼X	B'ST	ANC.	COLOR	X	DMC	¼X	ANC.	COLOR
	blanc		2	white		699			923	dk green		962		75	pink
	ecru		387	ecru		701			227	green		3716		25	lt pink
	310	/	403	black		702		/	226	lt green		3756		1037	lt baby blue
	321	/	9046	dk red		725			305	yellow		3766		167	aqua
	353		6	peach		754			1012	flesh		797		132	blue Fr. Knot
	433		358	dk brown		762			234	grey					
	435		1046	brown		775			128	baby blue					
	436		1045	tan		783		/	306	gold					
	437		362	lt tan		797		/	132	blue					
	666		46	red											

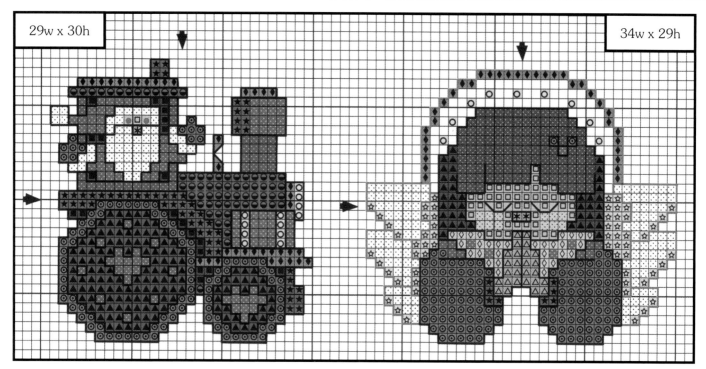

29w x 30h   34w x 29h

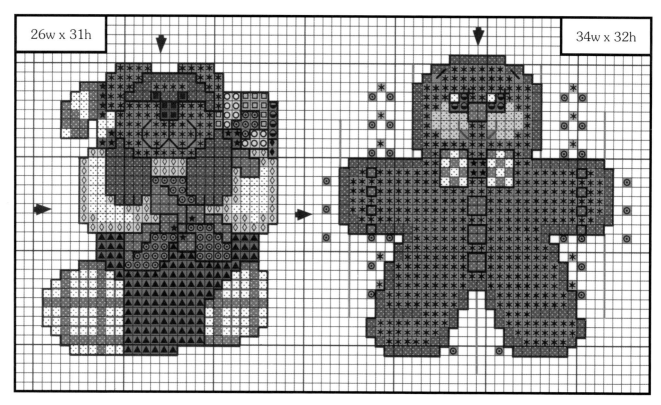

26w x 31h   34w x 32h

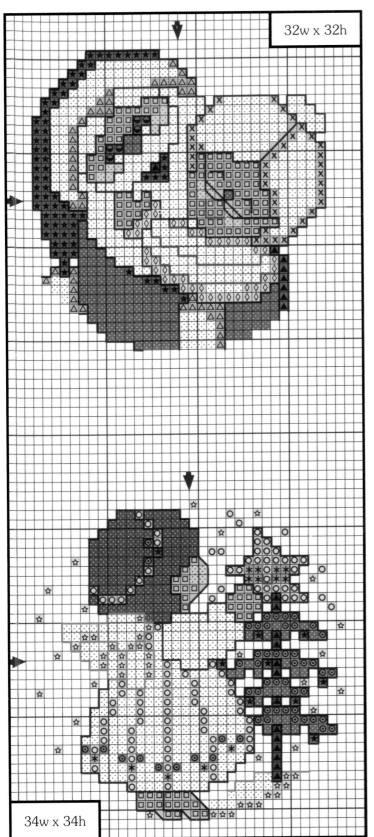

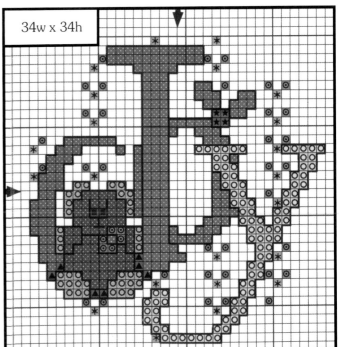

Each ornament on pages 66-69 was stitched on White Aida (18 ct) using 2 strands of floss for cross stitch and 1 strand for backstitch and French knots. Each design was inserted into an ornament frame.

BOOKMARKS

Shown on page 26. Charts continued on pages 72-73.

	Stitch Count: 26 wide x 99 high
1.	

	Stitch Count: 26 wide x 100 high
2.	

Cross Stitch – 2 strands

Symbol	Color	DMC	Anchor
·	white	blanc	2
♥	moss green	320	215
$	dk moss green	367	217
⊟	tan	436	1045
♦	dk red	498	1005
✧	bright green	704	256
✴	bright yellow	726	295
	yellow	743	302
▲	green	890	218
☆	yellow beige	3047	852
★	dk yellow green	3346	267
⊠	yellow green	3347	266
T	lt yellow green	3348	264
▼	brown	3371	382
■	dk rose	3687	68
◉	rose	3688	66
V	lt rose	3689	49
	fuchsia	3804	63

Backstitch – 1 strand

Symbol	Color
╱	bright green for #1
╱	green for #2
╱	fuchsia for flowers in #1
╱	brown for remaining backstitch

French Knot – 1 strand

Symbol	Color
○	yellow for flower centers in #1
◉	green for #2
●	brown for remaining French knots

Each Bookmark was stitched on a white or ecru prefinished bookmark (18 ct) using 2 strands of floss for cross stitch and 1 strand for backstitch and French knots. Each design size approximately 1¹/₂" x 5⁵/₈".

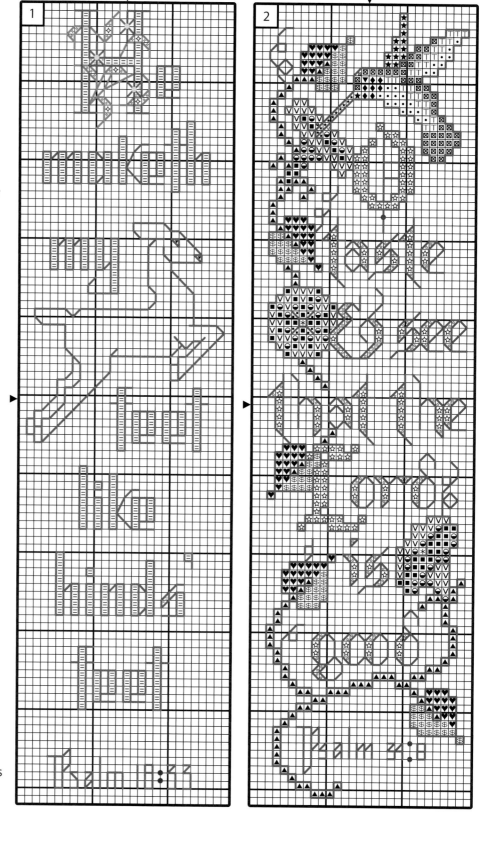

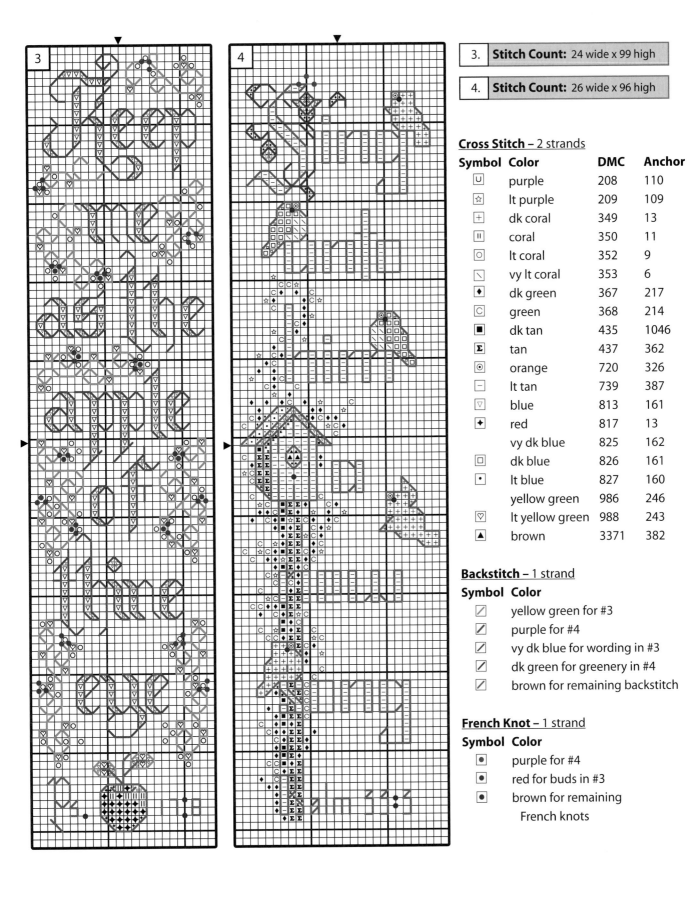

3. | **Stitch Count:** 24 wide x 99 high

4. | **Stitch Count:** 26 wide x 96 high

Cross Stitch – 2 strands

Symbol	Color	DMC	Anchor
U	purple	208	110
☆	lt purple	209	109
+	dk coral	349	13
ΙΙ	coral	350	11
○	lt coral	352	9
\	vy lt coral	353	6
◆	dk green	367	217
C	green	368	214
■	dk tan	435	1046
Σ	tan	437	362
◉	orange	720	326
–	lt tan	739	387
▽	blue	813	161
✦	red	817	13
	vy dk blue	825	162
□	dk blue	826	161
·	lt blue	827	160
	yellow green	986	246
♡	lt yellow green	988	243
▲	brown	3371	382

Backstitch – 1 strand

Symbol	Color
╱	yellow green for #3
╱	purple for #4
╱	vy dk blue for wording in #3
╱	dk green for greenery in #4
╱	brown for remaining backstitch

French Knot – 1 strand

Symbol	Color
●	purple for #4
●	red for buds in #3
●	brown for remaining French knots

BOOKMARKS (continued)

Shown on page 26.

5.	**Stitch Count:** 26 wide x 99 high

6.	**Stitch Count:** 25 wide x 100 high

Cross Stitch – 2 strands

Symbol	Color	DMC	Anchor
⊡	white	blanc	2
	brown	433	358
◉	gold	676	891
+	lt gold	677	886
☆	peach	754	1012
⊡	salmon	760	1022
	dk brown	898	360
	dk grey blue	930	1035
	grey blue	931	1034
✖	lt grey blue	932	1033
⊟	lt peach	948	1011
⊙	dk peach	950	4146
2	sky blue	3753	1031
■	vy dk peach	3773	1008

Backstitch – 1 strand

Symbol	Color
╱	dk grey blue
╱	dk brown for #6
╱	grey blue for wording in #5
╱	brown for remaining backstitch in #5

French Knot – 1 strand

Symbol	Color
●	dk brown for #6
●	grey blue for #5

Each Bookmark was stitched on a white or ecru prefinished bookmark (18 ct) using 2 strands of floss for cross stitch and 1 strand for backstitch and French knots. Each design size approximately 1¹/₂" x 5⁵/₈".

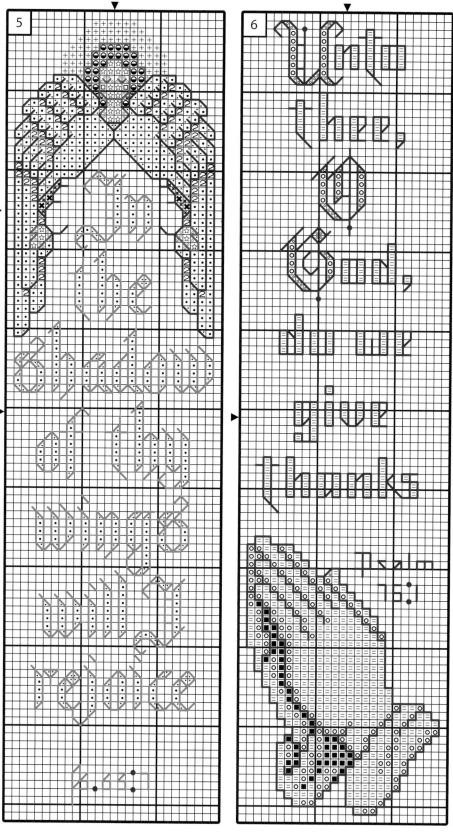

Cross Stitch – 2 strands

Symbol	Color	DMC	Anchor
⊟	ecru	ecru	387
▲	peach	353	6
V	green	367	217
Π	lt green	368	214
▣	purple	552	99
★	tan	738	361
◉	lt tan	739	387
◆	blue	796	133
■	brown	3371	382
	Kreinik (#8) Braid #002		

Backstitch – 1 strand

Symbol	Color
╱	Kreinik Fine (#8) Braid #002 for #7
╱	blue for wording in #7
╱	brown for #8

French Knot – 1 strand

Symbol	Color
◉	blue for #7
●	brown for #8

24w x 108h   26w x 107h   25w x 98h

The
Once upon a time
End
A good book is the best of friends

Each Novel Marker was stitched on a white prefinished bookmark (18 ct) using 2 strands of floss for cross stitch and 1 strand for backstitch and French knots. Each design size approximately 1½" x 6".

NOVEL MARKERS *Shown on page 27.*

X	DMC	¼X	¾X	B'ST	COLOR	X	DMC	¼X	B'ST	COLOR	X	DMC	¼X	B'ST	COLOR	X	DMC	COLOR
	blanc				white	C	721			orange	*	838			brown		326	dk pink French Knot
●	312				dk blue		743			yellow	V	910			dk green		743	yellow French Knot
◆	321				red		746			vy lt yellow		912			green	●	838	brown French Knot
—	326				dk pink	2	746			vy lt yellow	E	954			lt green	●	910	dk green French Knot
▲	334				blue	R	754			peach	■	3325			lt blue			
	335				pink	◆	782			dk gold	6	3326			lt pink			
						O	783			gold								

74

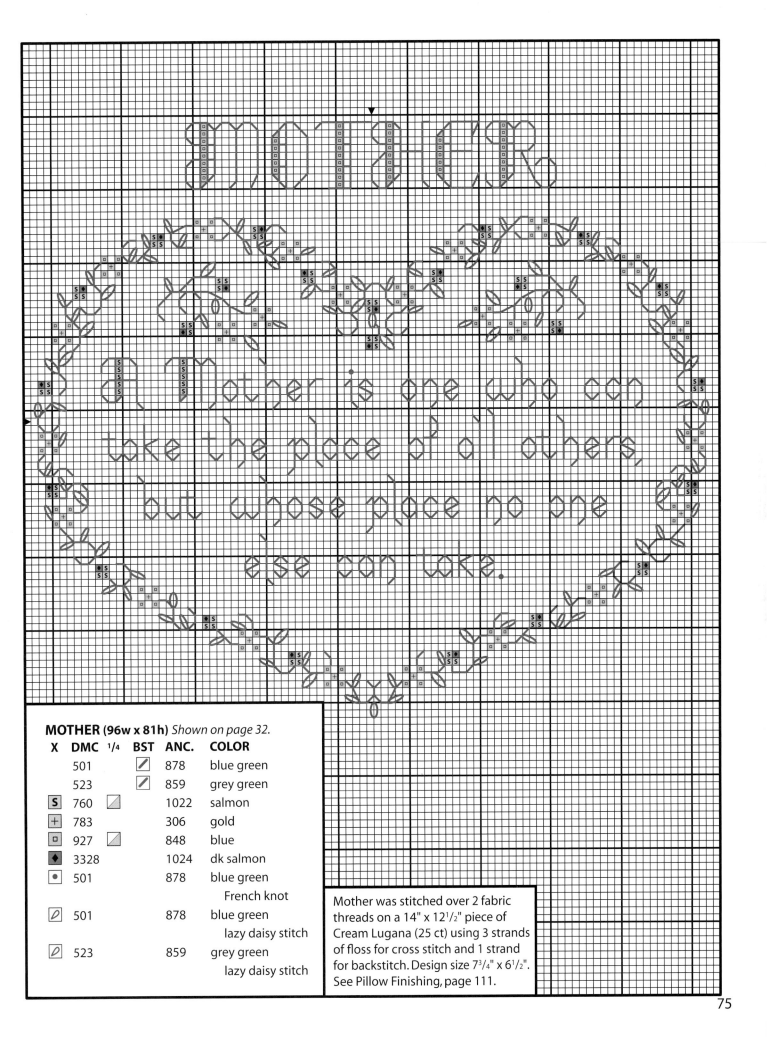

MOTHER (96w x 81h) *Shown on page 32.*

X	DMC	1/4	BST	ANC.	COLOR
	501		/	878	blue green
	523		/	859	grey green
S	760	◹		1022	salmon
+	783			306	gold
▫	927	◹		848	blue
◆	3328			1024	dk salmon
•	501			878	blue green
					French knot
⬭	501			878	blue green
					lazy daisy stitch
⬭	523			859	grey green
					lazy daisy stitch

Mother was stitched over 2 fabric threads on a 14" x 12¹/₂" piece of Cream Lugana (25 ct) using 3 strands of floss for cross stitch and 1 strand for backstitch. Design size 7³/₄" x 6¹/₂". See Pillow Finishing, page 111.

Center Name

You got it from your Father
it was all he had to give
So it's yours to use and cherish
for as long as you may live.
If you lose the watch he gave you
it can always be replaced;
but a black mark on your name
can never be erased.

It was clean the day you took it
and a worthy name to bear—
when he got it from his Father
there was no dishonor there.

So make sure you guard it wisely
after all is said and done.
You'll be glad the name is spotless
when you give it to your son.

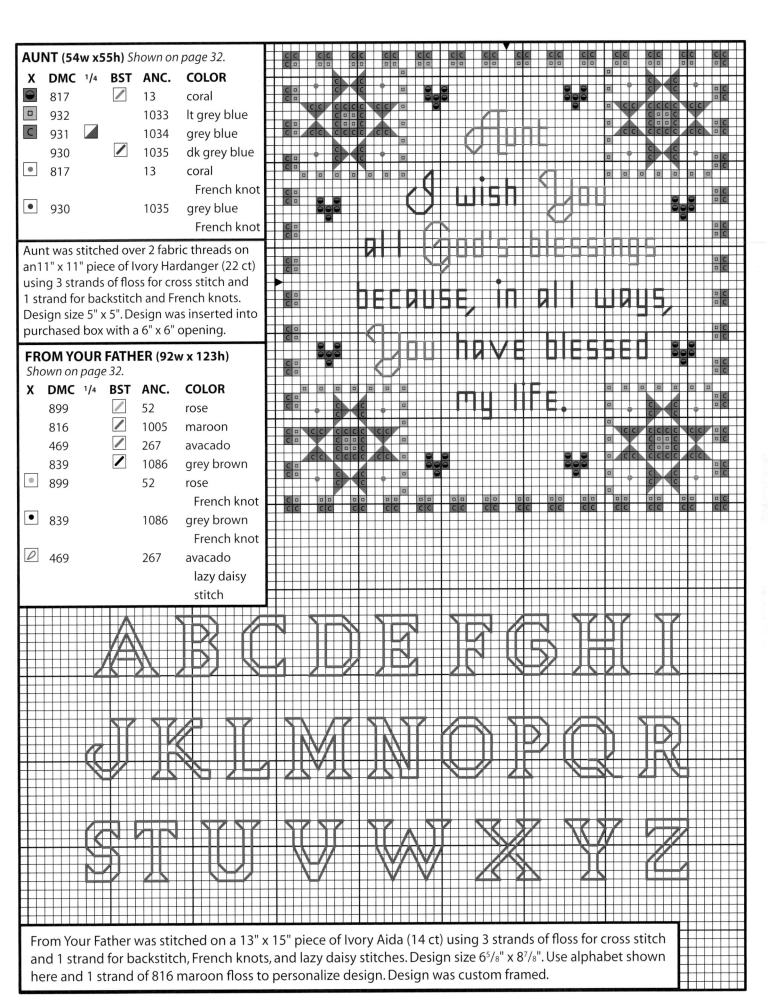

AUNT (54w x 55h) *Shown on page 32.*

X	DMC	1/4	BST	ANC.	COLOR
◑	817		╱	13	coral
▫	932			1033	lt grey blue
C	931	◣		1034	grey blue
	930		╱	1035	dk grey blue
•	817			13	coral French knot
●	930			1035	grey blue French knot

Aunt was stitched over 2 fabric threads on an 11" x 11" piece of Ivory Hardanger (22 ct) using 3 strands of floss for cross stitch and 1 strand for backstitch and French knots. Design size 5" x 5". Design was inserted into purchased box with a 6" x 6" opening.

FROM YOUR FATHER (92w x 123h)
Shown on page 32.

X	DMC	1/4	BST	ANC.	COLOR
	899		╱	52	rose
	816		╱	1005	maroon
	469		╱	267	avacado
	839		╱	1086	grey brown
•	899			52	rose French knot
●	839			1086	grey brown French knot
⬭	469			267	avacado lazy daisy stitch

From Your Father was stitched on a 13" x 15" piece of Ivory Aida (14 ct) using 3 strands of floss for cross stitch and 1 strand for backstitch, French knots, and lazy daisy stitches. Design size 6⅝" x 8⅞". Use alphabet shown here and 1 strand of 816 maroon floss to personalize design. Design was custom framed.

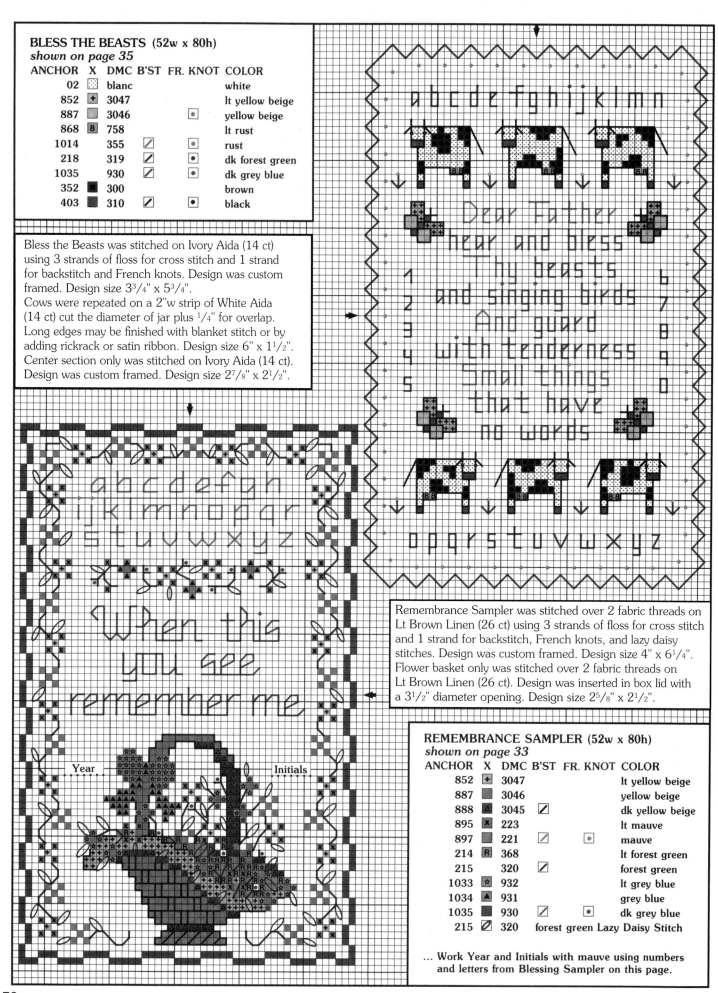

BLESS THE BEASTS (52w x 80h)
shown on page 35

ANCHOR	X	DMC	B'ST	FR. KNOT	COLOR
02		blanc			white
852	+	3047			lt yellow beige
887		3046		•	yellow beige
868	8	758			lt rust
1014		355	/	•	rust
218		319	/	•	dk forest green
1035		930	/	•	dk grey blue
352	■	300			brown
403	■	310	/	•	black

Bless the Beasts was stitched on Ivory Aida (14 ct) using 3 strands of floss for cross stitch and 1 strand for backstitch and French knots. Design was custom framed. Design size 3³/₄" x 5³/₄".
Cows were repeated on a 2"w strip of White Aida (14 ct) cut the diameter of jar plus ¹/₄" for overlap. Long edges may be finished with blanket stitch or by adding rickrack or satin ribbon. Design size 6" x 1¹/₂".
Center section only was stitched on Ivory Aida (14 ct). Design was custom framed. Design size 2⁷/₈" x 2¹/₂".

Remembrance Sampler was stitched over 2 fabric threads on Lt Brown Linen (26 ct) using 3 strands of floss for cross stitch and 1 strand for backstitch, French knots, and lazy daisy stitches. Design was custom framed. Design size 4" x 6¹/₄".
Flower basket only was stitched over 2 fabric threads on Lt Brown Linen (26 ct). Design was inserted in box lid with a 3¹/₂" diameter opening. Design size 2⁵/₈" x 2¹/₂".

REMEMBRANCE SAMPLER (52w x 80h)
shown on page 33

ANCHOR	X	DMC	B'ST	FR. KNOT	COLOR
852	+	3047			lt yellow beige
887		3046			yellow beige
888	▲	3045	/		dk yellow beige
895	X	223			lt mauve
897		221	/	•	mauve
214	R	368	/		lt forest green
215		320	/		forest green
1033	☆	932			lt grey blue
1034	▲	931			grey blue
1035	■	930	/	•	dk grey blue
215	/	320			forest green Lazy Daisy Stitch

... Work Year and Initials with mauve using numbers and letters from Blessing Sampler on this page.

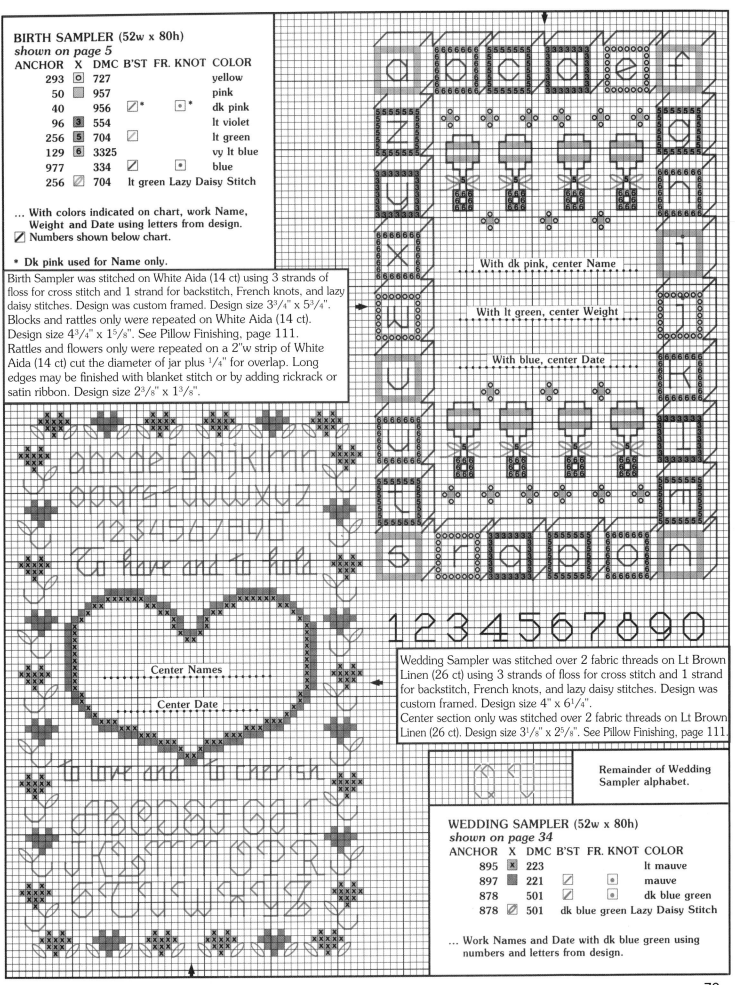

BIRTH SAMPLER (52w x 80h)
shown on page 5

ANCHOR	X	DMC	B'ST	FR. KNOT	COLOR
293	⊙	727			yellow
50	▦	957			pink
40		956	▨*	⊡*	dk pink
96	3	554			lt violet
256	5	704	▨		lt green
129	6	3325			vy lt blue
977		334	▨	⊡	blue
256	▨	704			lt green Lazy Daisy Stitch

... With colors indicated on chart, work Name, Weight and Date using letters from design.
▨ Numbers shown below chart.

* Dk pink used for Name only.

Birth Sampler was stitched on White Aida (14 ct) using 3 strands of floss for cross stitch and 1 strand for backstitch, French knots, and lazy daisy stitches. Design was custom framed. Design size 3³/₄" x 5³/₄". Blocks and rattles only were repeated on White Aida (14 ct). Design size 4³/₄" x 1⁵/₈". See Pillow Finishing, page 111. Rattles and flowers only were repeated on a 2"w strip of White Aida (14 ct) cut the diameter of jar plus ¹/₄" for overlap. Long edges may be finished with blanket stitch or by adding rickrack or satin ribbon. Design size 2³/₈" x 1³/₈".

With dk pink, center Name

With lt green, center Weight

With blue, center Date

Center Names

Center Date

Wedding Sampler was stitched over 2 fabric threads on Lt Brown Linen (26 ct) using 3 strands of floss for cross stitch and 1 strand for backstitch, French knots, and lazy daisy stitches. Design was custom framed. Design size 4" x 6¹/₄".
Center section only was stitched over 2 fabric threads on Lt Brown Linen (26 ct). Design size 3¹/₈" x 2⁵/₈". See Pillow Finishing, page 111.

Remainder of Wedding Sampler alphabet.

WEDDING SAMPLER (52w x 80h)
shown on page 34

ANCHOR	X	DMC	B'ST	FR. KNOT	COLOR
895	✕	223			lt mauve
897	▦	221	▨	⊡	mauve
878		501	▨	⊡	dk blue green
878	▨	501			dk blue green Lazy Daisy Stitch

... Work Names and Date with dk blue green using numbers and letters from design.

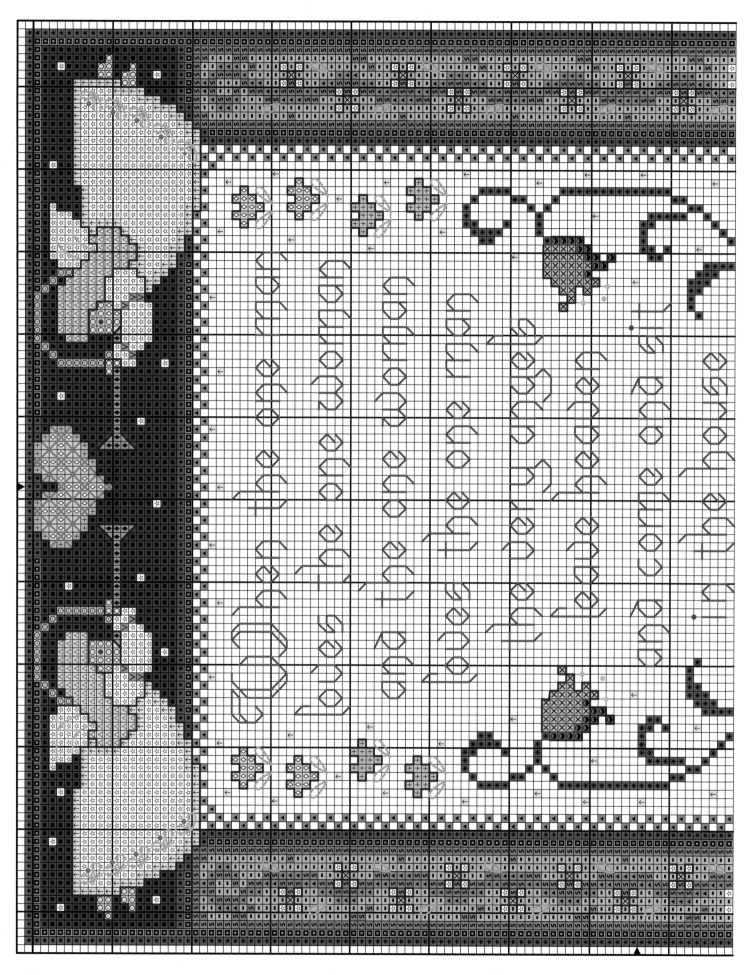

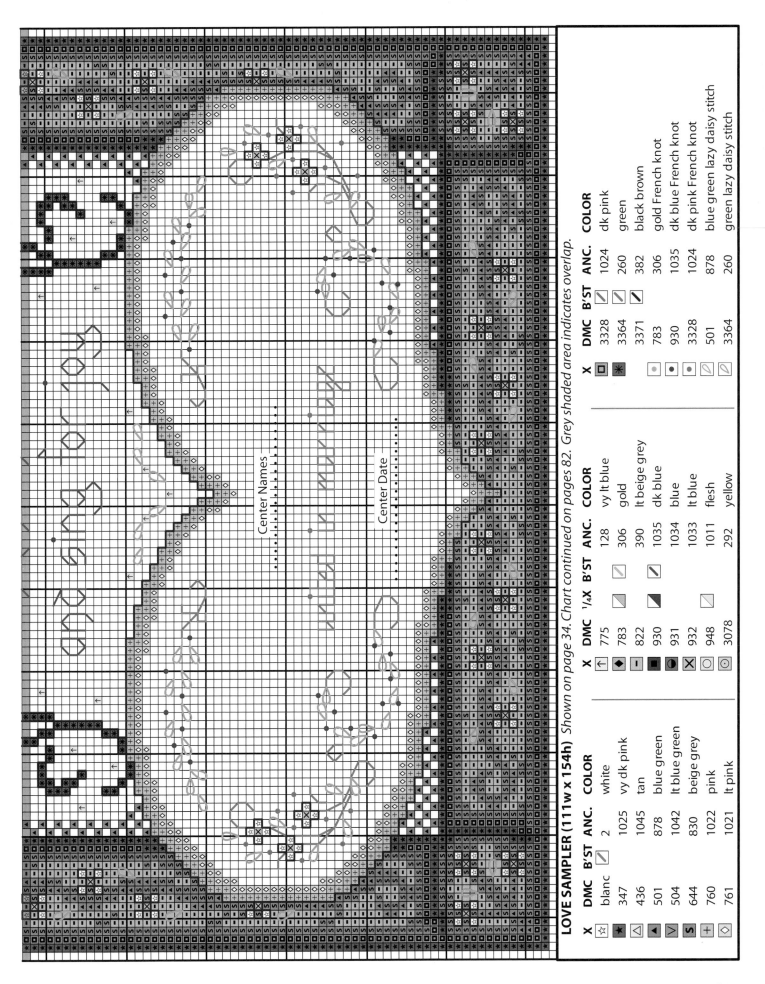

LOVE SAMPLER (111w x 154h) *Shown on page 34. Chart continued on pages 82. Grey shaded area indicates overlap.*

X	DMC	B'ST	ANC.	COLOR
☆	blanc	◩	2	white
★	347		1025	vy dk pink
◁	436		1045	tan
◀	501		878	blue green
▷	504		1042	lt blue green
S	644		830	beige grey
+	760		1022	pink
◇	761		1021	lt pink

X	DMC	¹/₄X	B'ST	ANC.	COLOR
←	775			128	vy lt blue
◆	783	◪		306	gold
❙	822	◪		390	lt beige grey
■	930	◪	◩	1035	dk blue
◐	931			1034	blue
✕	932			1033	lt blue
○	948	◪		1011	flesh
⊙	3078			292	yellow

X	DMC	B'ST	ANC.	COLOR
▢	3328	◪	1024	dk pink
✳	3364	◪	260	green
	3371	◪	382	black brown
●	783		306	gold French knot
●	930		1035	dk blue French knot
●	3328		1024	dk pink French knot
◪	501		878	blue green lazy daisy stitch
◪	3364		260	green lazy daisy stitch

Center Names

Center Date

81

LOVE SAMPLER
(chart on pages
80–81) was stitched
over 2 fabric threads
on a 15" x 18½" piece
of Cream Lugana
(25 ct) using 3 strands
of floss for cross stitch
and 1 strand for
backstitch, French
knots, and lazy
daisy stitches. Use
alphabet shown
here and 1 strand of
930 dk blue floss to
personalize sampler.
Sampler design size
8⅞" x 12⅜". Design
was custom framed.

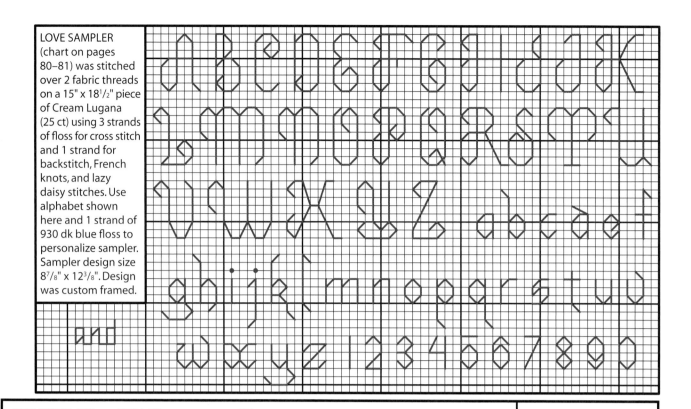

TEACHER (83w x 51h) *Shown on page 28.*

X	DMC	¼X	B'ST	ANC.	COLOR
⬚	blanc			2	white
◆	304		☑	1006	lt red
▢	320			215	lt grey green
▲	336			150	navy
◉	367			217	grey green
◆	433			358	brown
✕	680	◪		901	dk gold
V	729	◹	☑	890	gold
+	738			361	lt tan

X	DMC	¼X	B'ST	ANC.	COLOR
▨	739			387	vy lt tan
✻	801	◪		359	dk brown
◆	815			43	dk red
◙	890			218	dk grey green
★	930		☑	1035	dk grey blue
✕	931			1034	grey blue
▣	932			1033	lt grey blue
	3371		☑	382	brown black
⊙	930			1035	dk grey blue Fr. Knot

TEACHER was stitched over 2 fabric threads on a 13" x 10½" piece of Ivory Lugana (25 ct) using 3 strands of floss for cross stitch and 1 strand for backstitch and French knots. Design size 6¾" x 4⅛". Design was custom framed.

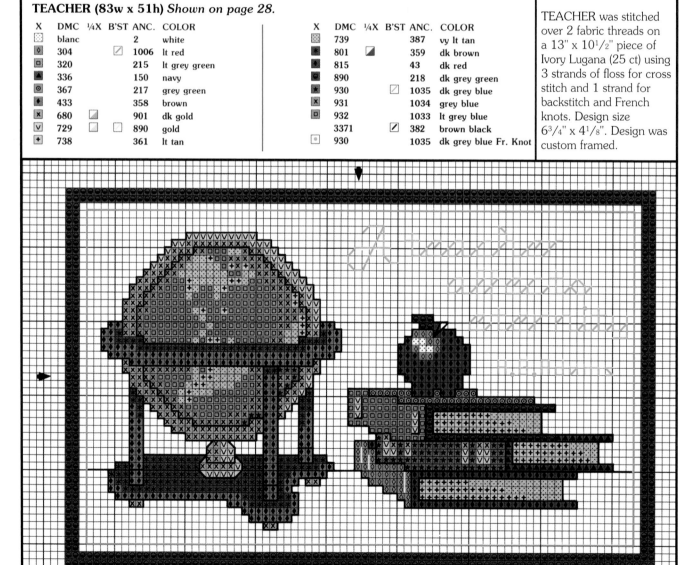

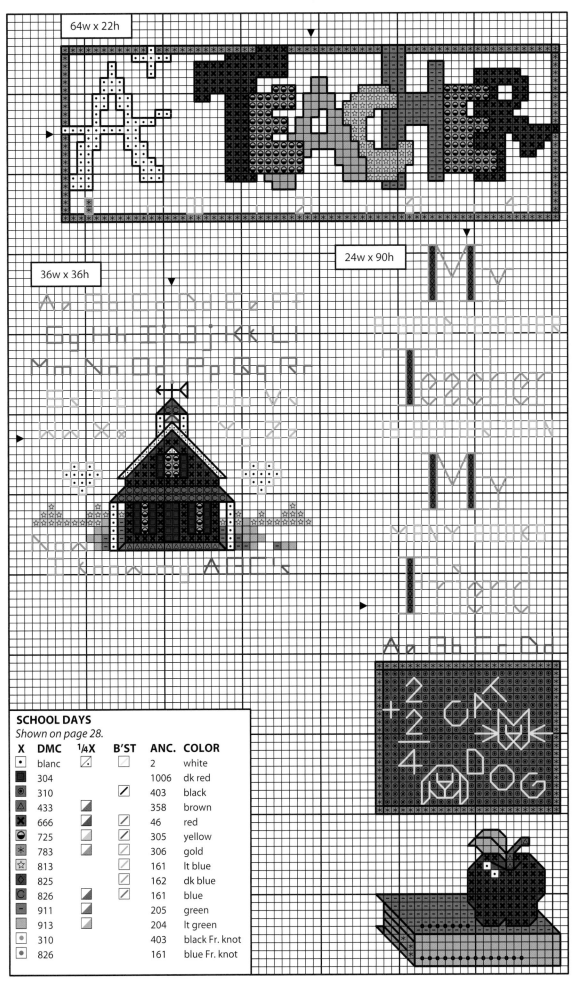

A+ Teacher was stitched on a 9" x 6" piece of Black Aida (14 ct) using 4 strands of floss for cross stitch and 1 for backstitch. Design size 4⅝" x 1⅝". Design was mounted on cardboard and glued to a blackboard eraser.

Schoolhouse Sampler was stitched on a 9" x 9" piece of White Aida (14 ct) using 3 strands of floss for cross stitch and 1 strand for backstitch and French knots. Design size 2⅝" x 2⅝". Design was custom framed.

My Teacher, My Friend was stitched on a white prefinished bookmark (18 ct) using 2 strands of floss for cross stitch and 1 strand for backstitch. Backstitch name on dotted lines on book with 1 strand of 310 black floss using alphabet from Schoolhouse Sampler. Design size 1⅜" x 5".

64w x 22h

36w x 36h

24w x 90h

SCHOOL DAYS
Shown on page 28.

X	DMC	¼X	B'ST	ANC.	COLOR
•	blanc	◪	◪	2	white
■	304			1006	dk red
◉	310		◪	403	black
△	433	◪		358	brown
✕	666	◪	◪	46	red
◓	725	◪	◪	305	yellow
✳	783	◪	◪	306	gold
☆	813		◪	161	lt blue
◈	825		◪	162	dk blue
◖	826	◪	◪	161	blue
–	911	◪		205	green
	913	◪		204	lt green
⦿	310			403	black Fr. knot
⦿	826			161	blue Fr. knot

83

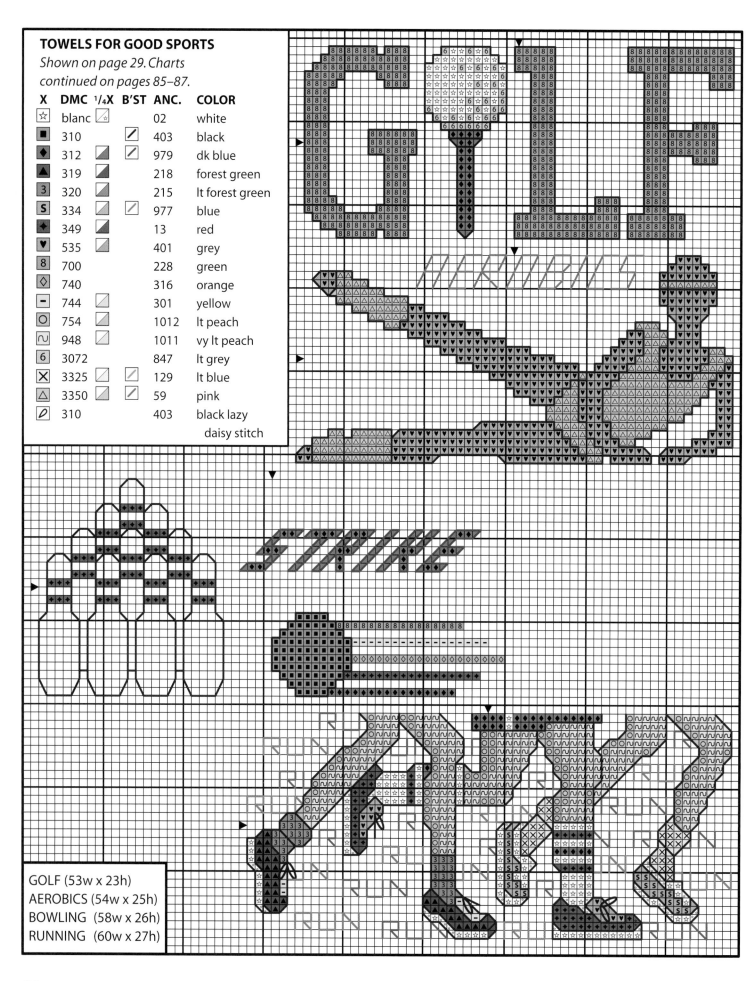

TOWELS FOR GOOD SPORTS

Shown on page 29. Charts
continued on pages 85–87.

Charts continued on pages 85–87.

X	DMC	¼X	B'ST	ANC.	COLOR
☆	blanc			02	white
■	310		╱	403	black
◆	312	◣	╱	979	dk blue
▲	319	◣		218	forest green
3	320	◣		215	lt forest green
S	334	◣	╱	977	blue
◆	349	◣		13	red
♥	535	◣		401	grey
8	700			228	green
◇	740			316	orange
-	744	◣		301	yellow
O	754	◣		1012	lt peach
∩	948	◣		1011	vy lt peach
6	3072			847	lt grey
X	3325	◣	╱	129	lt blue
△	3350	◣	╱	59	pink
╱	310			403	black lazy
					daisy stitch

GOLF (53w x 23h)
AEROBICS (54w x 25h)
BOWLING (58w x 26h)
RUNNING (60w x 27h)

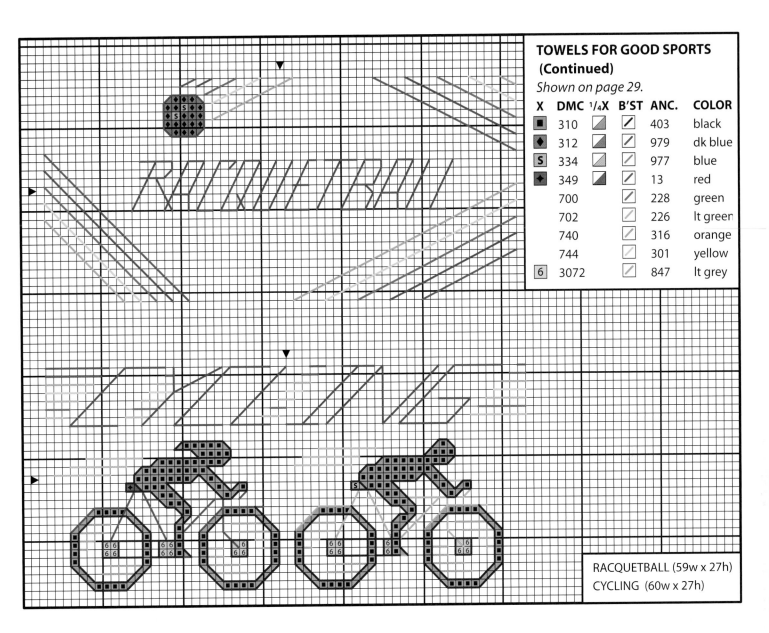

X	DMC	1/4X	B'ST	ANC.	COLOR
■	310	◹	◹	403	black
◆	312	◹	◹	979	dk blue
S	334	◹	◹	977	blue
✦	349	◹	◹	13	red
	700		◹	228	green
	702		◹	226	lt green
	740		◹	316	orange
	744		◹	301	yellow
6	3072		◹	847	lt grey

RACQUETBALL (59w x 27h)
CYCLING (60w x 27h)

Each design on pages 84–87, Towels for Good Sports, was stitched on a prefinished hand towel with an Aida (14 ct) insert using 3 stands of floss for cross stitch, 2 strands for backstitched letters, and 1 strand for lazy daisy stitches and remaining backstitch.

Design	Color of Towel	Design Size
Aerobics	Light Rose	$3^7/_8" \times 1^7/_8"$
Baseball	White	$4^3/_8" \times 2"$
Basketball	White	$4^3/_8" \times 2"$
Body Building	White	$4^3/_8" \times 2"$
Bowling	White	$4^1/_4" \times 1^7/_8"$
Cycling	White	$4^3/_8" \times 2"$
Golf	Blue Ridge	$3^7/_8" \times 1^3/_4"$
Racquetball	White	$4^1/_4" \times 2"$
Running	White	$4^3/_8" \times 2"$
Soccer	Yellow	$4^3/_8" \times 2"$
Tennis	Peach	$4^3/_8" \times 2"$

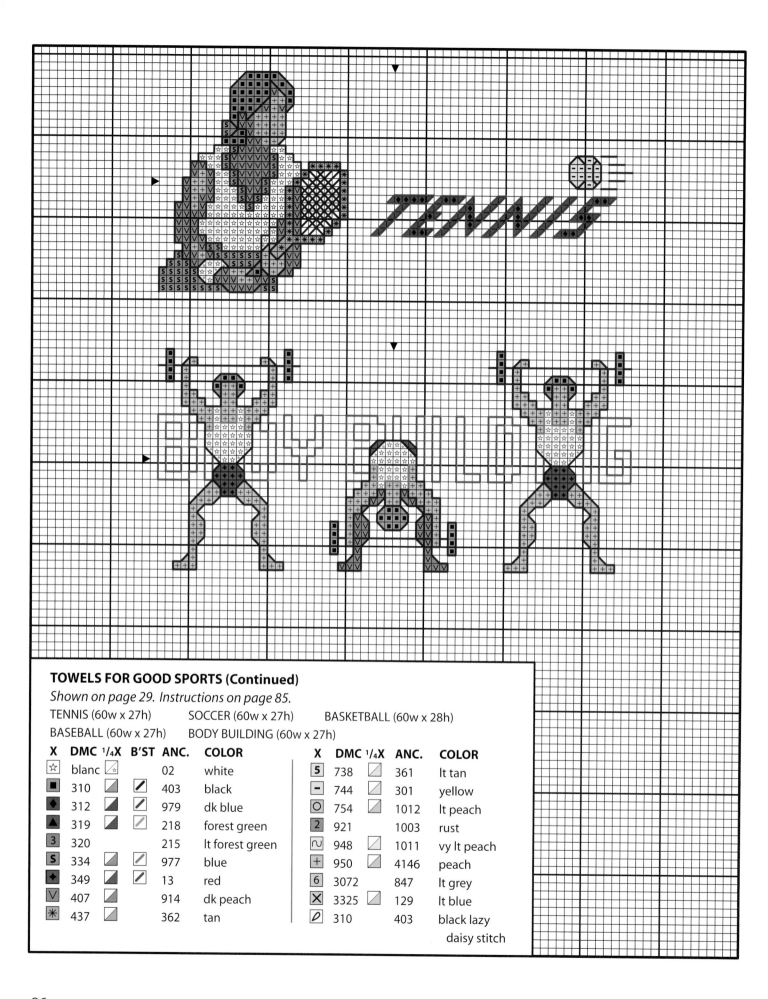

TOWELS FOR GOOD SPORTS (Continued)

Shown on page 29. Instructions on page 85.

TENNIS (60w x 27h)   SOCCER (60w x 27h)   BASKETBALL (60w x 28h)
BASEBALL (60w x 27h)   BODY BUILDING (60w x 27h)

X	DMC	¼X	B'ST	ANC.	COLOR		X	DMC	¼X	ANC.	COLOR
☆	blanc	◪		02	white		5	738	◪	361	lt tan
■	310	◪	◪	403	black		-	744	◪	301	yellow
◆	312	◪	◪	979	dk blue		O	754	◪	1012	lt peach
▲	319	◪	◪	218	forest green		2	921		1003	rust
3	320			215	lt forest green		∩	948	◪	1011	vy lt peach
S	334	◪	◪	977	blue		+	950	◪	4146	peach
◆	349	◪	◪	13	red		6	3072		847	lt grey
V	407	◪		914	dk peach		X	3325	◪	129	lt blue
✳	437	◪		362	tan		∅	310		403	black lazy
											daisy stitch

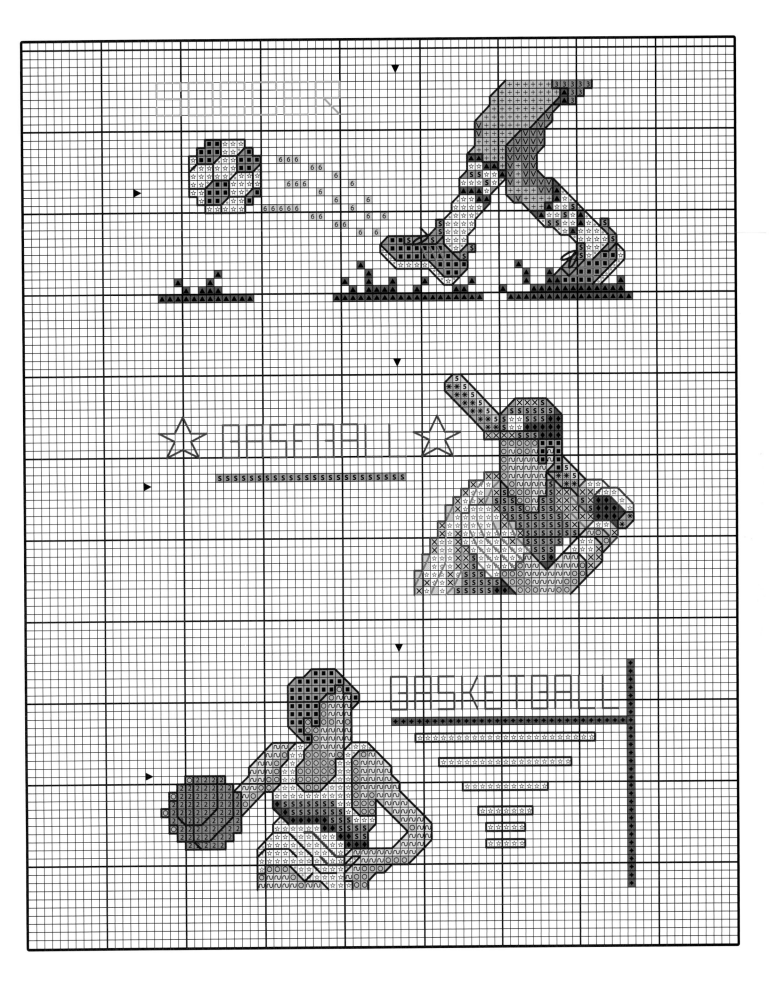

CAROUSEL HORSE (100w x 87h) *Shown on page 30.*

X	DMC	¼X	B'ST	ANC.	COLOR
░	blanc	░		2	white
-	ecru	☐		387	ecru
	326		◢	59	dk pink
◆	335			38	pink
	349		◢	13	coral
◉	352			9	dk peach
✦	353			6	peach
✳	407	◢		914	dk rose brown
▨	543	◢		933	vy lt beige brown
▲	632	◢		936	vy dk rose brown

X	DMC		¼X	B'ST	ANC.	COLOR
◉	725 & 002	*		◢	305	yellow
◉	726 & 002	*			295	lt yellow
◈	754				1012	lt peach
★	783 & 002	*			306	dk gold
	796			◢	133	vy dk blue
▨	798		◢		131	dk blue
✳	799		◢		136	blue
▨	800		◢		144	lt blue
	909			◢	923	dk green
★	911				205	lt green

X	DMC	¼X	B'ST	ANC.	COLOR
◉	912		◢	209	vy lt green
△	950			4146	lt rose brown
☐	3326			36	lt pink
	3371		◢	382	brown black
■	3799	◢	◢	236	vy dk grey

* Kreinik Blending Filament #002 gold

CAROUSEL HORSE
14 count	7¼"	x	6¼"	
16 count	6¼"	x	5½"	
18 count	5⅝"	x	4⅞"	
22 count	4⅝"	x	4"	

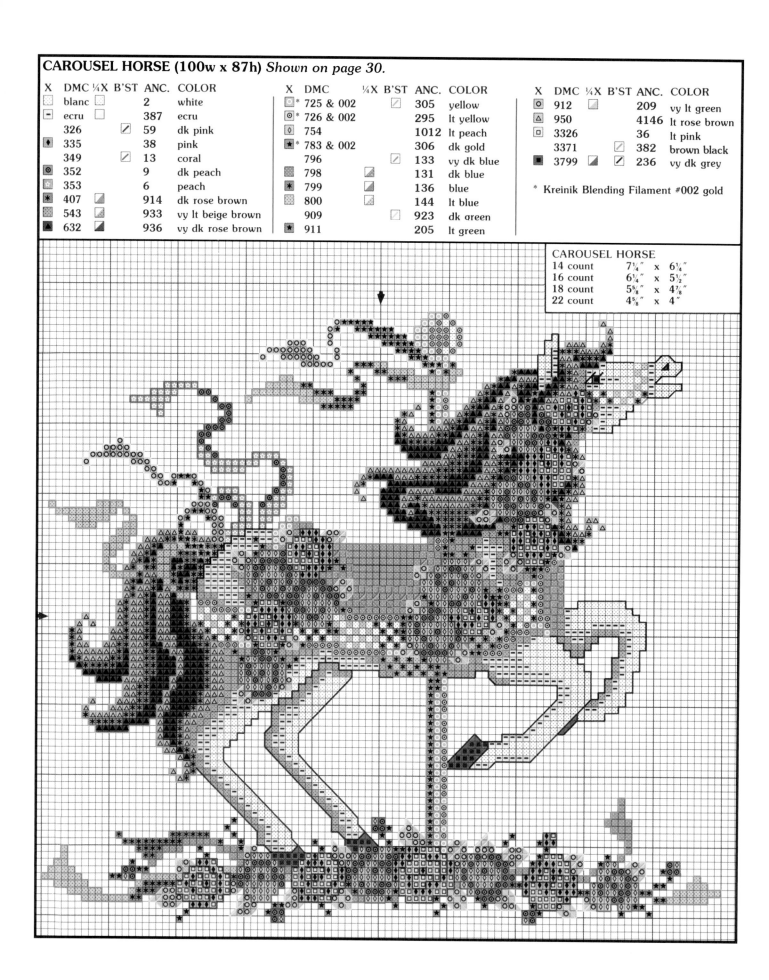

Carousel Horse was stitched on a 13½" x 12½" piece of Antique White Aida (14 ct) using 3 strands of floss for cross stitch and 1 strand for backstitch. For floss blended with blending filament, 3 strands of floss and 1 strand of blending filament were used for cross stitch and 1 strand of each was used for backstitch. Design size 7¼" x 6¼". Design was custom framed

Head #1 (design size 3¼" x 3") and Head #2 (design size 3¼" x 3") were stitched on a 14" x 9" piece of Antique White Aida (14 ct) leaving 1" between designs and using 3 strands of floss for cross stitch and 1 strand for backstitch. For floss blended with blending filament, 3 strands of floss and 1 strand of blending filament were used for cross stitch and 1 strand of each were used for backstitch. Design size (as shown on page 30) 7¾" x 3". See Pillow Finishing, page 111.

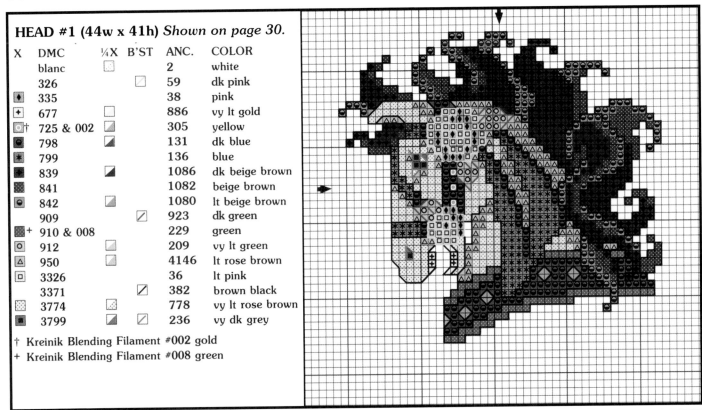

HEAD #1 (44w x 41h) *Shown on page 30.*

X	DMC	¼X	B'ST	ANC.	COLOR
	blanc			2	white
	326			59	dk pink
	335			38	pink
	677			886	vy lt gold
	725 & 002			305	yellow
	798			131	dk blue
	799			136	blue
	839			1086	dk beige brown
	841			1082	beige brown
	842			1080	lt beige brown
	909			923	dk green
	910 & 008			229	green
	912			209	vy lt green
	950			4146	lt rose brown
	3326			36	lt pink
	3371			382	brown black
	3774			778	vy lt rose brown
	3799			236	vy dk grey

† Kreinik Blending Filament #002 gold
+ Kreinik Blending Filament #008 green

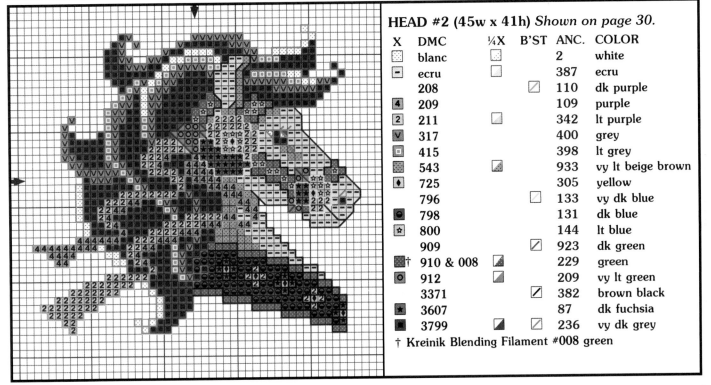

HEAD #2 (45w x 41h) *Shown on page 30.*

X	DMC	¼X	B'ST	ANC.	COLOR
	blanc			2	white
	ecru			387	ecru
	208			110	dk purple
	209			109	purple
	211			342	lt purple
	317			400	grey
	415			398	lt grey
	543			933	vy lt beige brown
	725			305	yellow
	796			133	vy dk blue
	798			131	dk blue
	800			144	lt blue
	909			923	dk green
	910 & 008			229	green
	912			209	vy lt green
	3371			382	brown black
	3607			87	dk fuchsia
	3799			236	vy dk grey

† Kreinik Blending Filament #008 green

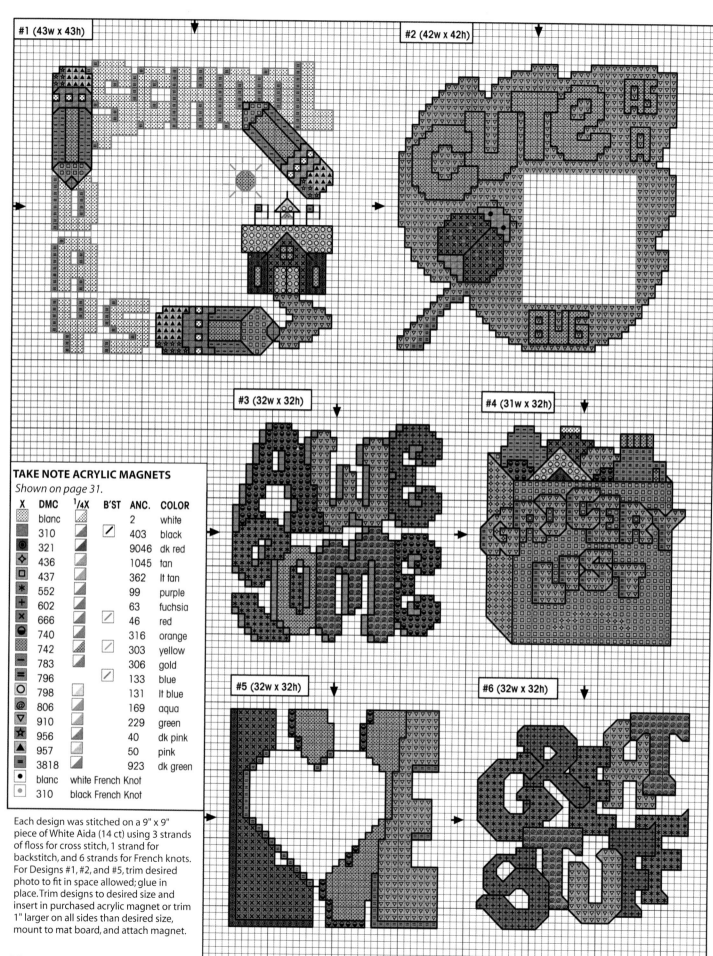

TAKE NOTE ACRYLIC MAGNETS

Shown on page 31.

X	DMC	¼X	B'ST	ANC.	COLOR
	blanc			2	white
	310		/	403	black
	321			9046	dk red
	436			1045	tan
	437			362	lt tan
	552			99	purple
	602			63	fuchsia
	666		/	46	red
	740			316	orange
	742		/	303	yellow
	783			306	gold
	796		/	133	blue
	798			131	lt blue
	806			169	aqua
	910			229	green
	956			40	dk pink
	957			50	pink
	3818			923	dk green
	blanc				white French Knot
	310				black French Knot

Each design was stitched on a 9" x 9" piece of White Aida (14 ct) using 3 strands of floss for cross stitch, 1 strand for backstitch, and 6 strands for French knots. For Designs #1, #2, and #5, trim desired photo to fit in space allowed; glue in place. Trim designs to desired size and insert in purchased acrylic magnet or trim 1" larger on all sides than desired size, mount to mat board, and attach magnet.

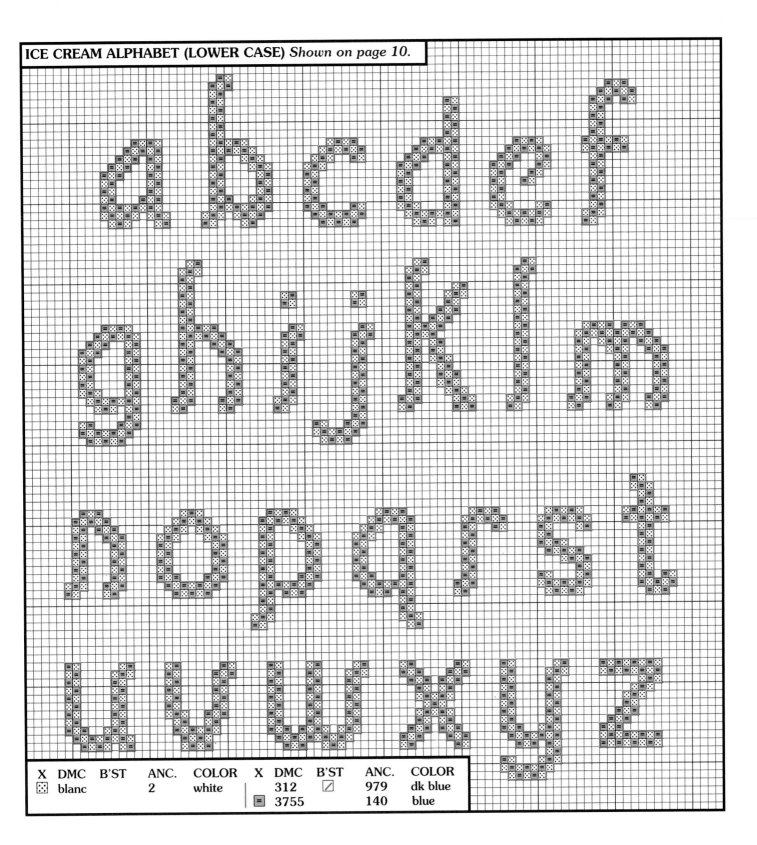

X	DMC	B'ST	ANC.	COLOR	X	DMC	B'ST	ANC.	COLOR
⊡	blanc		2	white		312	◸	979	dk blue
					▣	3755		140	blue

Children's Alphabets on pages 91–95 may be used to
stitch initials, names, or a favorite saying or phrase on
evenweave fabric, on items prefinished for cross stitch,
or over waste canvas on purchased garments. A grid is
provided on page 112 for charting desired letters.

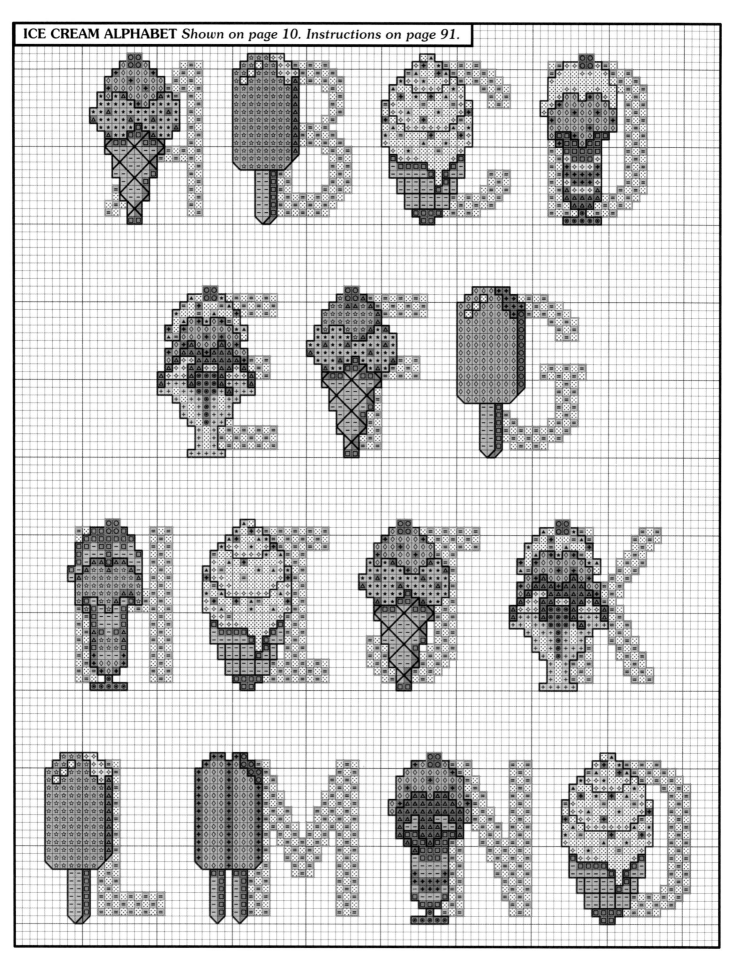

ICE CREAM ALPHABET *Shown on page 10. Instructions on page 91.*

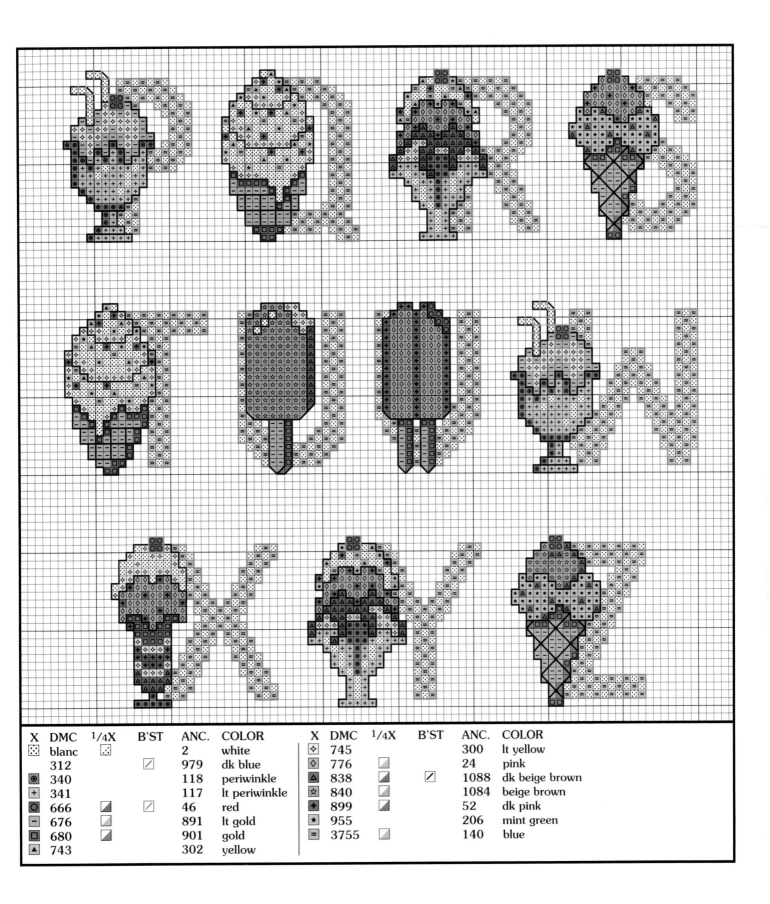

X	DMC	1/4X	B'ST	ANC.	COLOR		X	DMC	1/4X	B'ST	ANC.	COLOR
⊡	blanc	⊡		2	white		✦	745			300	lt yellow
	312		╱	979	dk blue		◇	776	╱		24	pink
◉	340			118	periwinkle		▲	838	╱	╱	1088	dk beige brown
✚	341			117	lt periwinkle		☆	840	╱		1084	beige brown
◎	666	╱	╱	46	red		✦	899	╱		52	dk pink
−	676	╱		891	lt gold		★	955			206	mint green
▣	680	╱		901	gold		=	3755	╱		140	blue
▲	743			302	yellow							

93

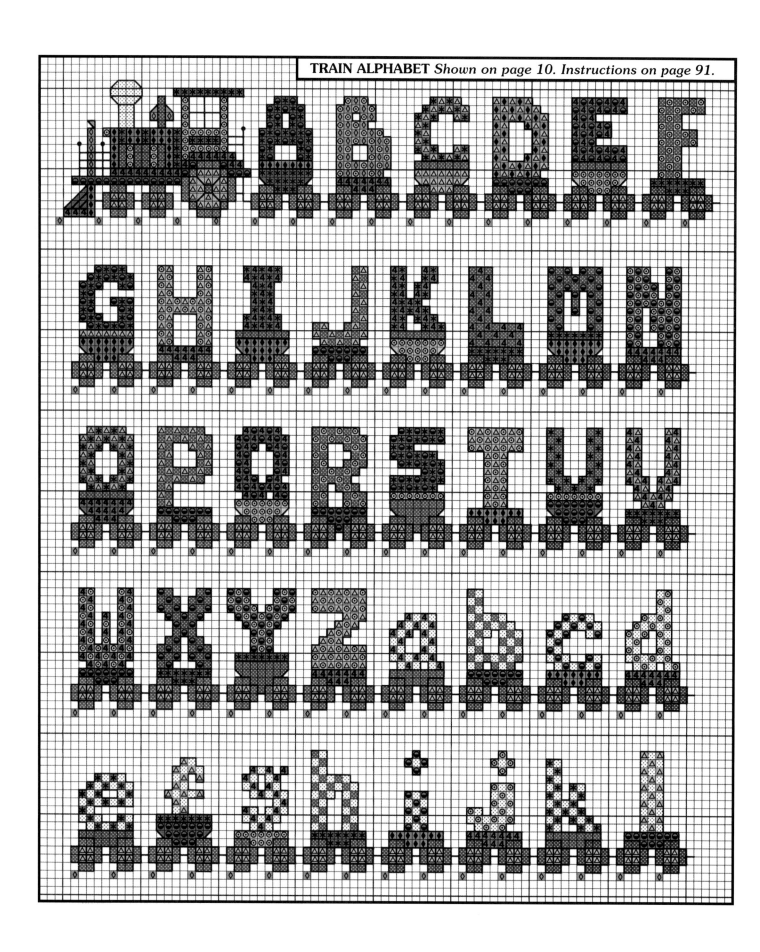

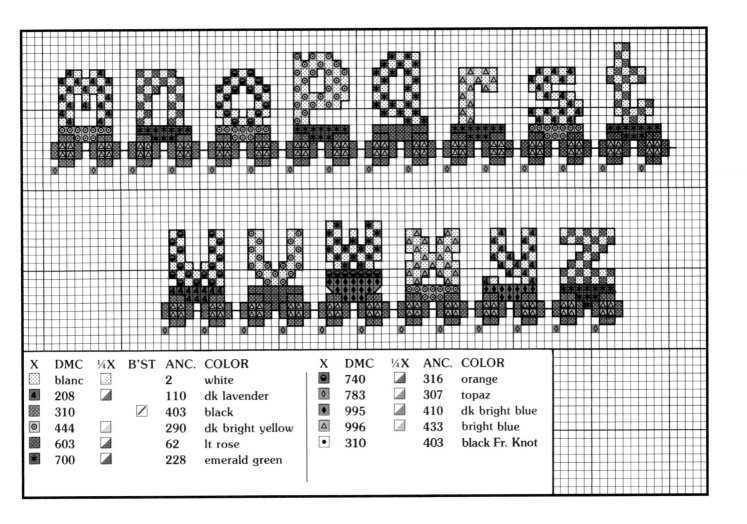

X	DMC	¼X	B'ST	ANC.	COLOR		X	DMC	¼X	ANC.	COLOR
	blanc			2	white			740		316	orange
	208			110	dk lavender			783		307	topaz
	310			403	black			995		410	dk bright blue
	444			290	dk bright yellow			996		433	bright blue
	603			62	lt rose			310		403	black Fr. Knot
	700			228	emerald green						

Baby Sampler (chart on pages 96–97) was stitched on a 15¹⁄₂" x 18¹⁄₂" piece of Antique White Aida (14 ct) using 3 strands of floss for cross stitch and 1 strand for backstitch. Design size 9¹⁄₄" x 12¹⁄₈". Design was custom framed.

ALPHABET FOR BABY SAMPLER *(pages 96-97)*

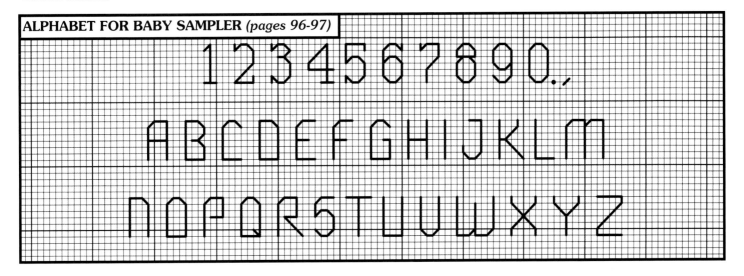

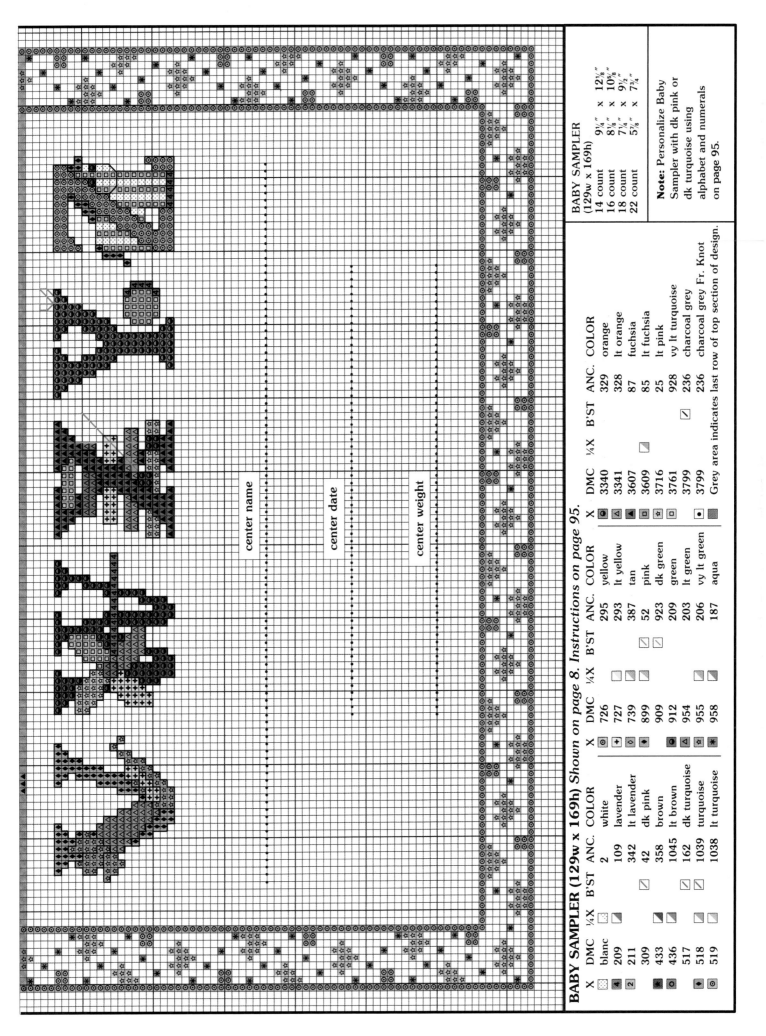

BABY SAMPLER (129w x 169h) Shown on page 8. Instructions on page 95.

center name

center date

center weight

X	DMC	¼X	B'ST	ANC.	COLOR
	blanc			2	white
◢	209			109	lavender
◿	211			342	lt lavender
	309		◹		dk pink
✱	433			358	brown
◯	436			1045	lt brown
	517		◹	162	dk turquoise
◆	518		◹	1039	turquoise
◉	519		◹	1038	lt turquoise

X	DMC	¼X	B'ST	ANC.	COLOR
◉	726			295	yellow
✚	727	◻		293	lt yellow
◈	739	◿		387	tan
◆	899	◣		52	pink
◐	909		◻	923	dk green
◑	912		◻	209	green
◿	954	◿		203	lt green
☆	955			206	vy lt green
✶	958	◣		187	aqua

X	DMC	¼X	B'ST	ANC.	COLOR
◐	3340			329	orange
◁	3341			328	lt orange
◀	3607			87	fuchsia
◻	3609			85	lt fuchsia
✿	3716			25	lt pink
◻	3761			928	vy lt turquoise
●	3799		◹	236	charcoal grey
▩	3799			236	charcoal grey Fr. Knot

Grey area indicates last row of top section of design.

Instructions on page 95.

BABY SAMPLER
(129w x 169h)

14 count	9¼"	x	12⅛"
16 count	8⅛"	x	10⅝"
18 count	7¼"	x	9½"
22 count	5⅞"	x	7¾"

Note: Personalize Baby Sampler with dk pink or dk turquoise using alphabet and numerals on page 95.

BABY (191w x 40h) *Shown on page 7.*

X	DMC	¹⁄₄X	B'ST	ANC.	COLOR
·	blanc			2	white
	340			118	lavender
	435			1046	brown
	436			1045	lt brown
	518			1039	dk blue
	519			1038	blue
	676			891	gold
	677			886	lt gold
	742			303	orange
	745			300	yellow
	746			275	lt yellow
	898			360	dk brown
	954			203	green
	958			187	dk aqua
	959			186	aqua
	963			73	lt pink
	964			185	lt aqua
	3716			25	pink
	3747			120	lt lavender
	3761			928	lt blue

Note: *Stitch leaving nine squares between letters.*

Baby was stitched on White Aida (14 ct) using 3 strands of floss for cross stitch and 1 strand for backstitch. Design size 13³⁄₄" x 2⁷⁄₈". Design was custom framed.

Shows placement of previous letter.

BE HAPPY BIBS *Shown on page 6. Charts continued on pages 100–101.*

X	DMC	¼X	B'ST	ANC.	COLOR	X	DMC	¼X	B'ST	ANC.	COLOR	X	DMC	¼X	ANC.	COLOR
☆	blanc	◫		2	white	◇	519			1038	lt turquiose	◖	912		209	dk green
4	209			109	purple		550		╱	102	dk purple	∿	948	╱	1011	lt peach
2	210			108	lt purple	C	726	◫		295	yellow	◎	954		203	lt green
	309		╱	42	vy dk pink	A	727	◫		293	lt yellow	◙	959		186	aqua
■	310			403	black	♥	739	◫		387	tan	5	3326		36	pink
	312		╱	979	vy dk blue	◆	741	◫		304	bright orange	S	3340		329	orange
▲	322	◨		978	dk blue	△	754			1012	flesh	H	3341		328	lt orange
	349		╱	13	dk coral	✕	775			128	baby blue	◐	3706	◫	33	salmon
	433		╱	358	brown	▢	818			23	lt pink	V	3708		31	lt salmon
O	437	◨		362	lt brown	B	899			52	dk pink	✳	3755		140	blue
	517		╱	162	dk turquoise		900		╱	333	dk burnt orange	R	3756		1037	lt baby blue
★	518		╱	1039	turquoise		909		╱	923	vy dk green					

Hatching Out (design size 5⅞" x 2¼") and Clown (design size 5"x 2¼") were stitched on white velour baby bibs with Aida (14 ct) inserts using 3 strands of floss for cross stitch and 1 for backstitch.

HATCHING OUT (82w x 30h)

CLOWN (70w x 30h)

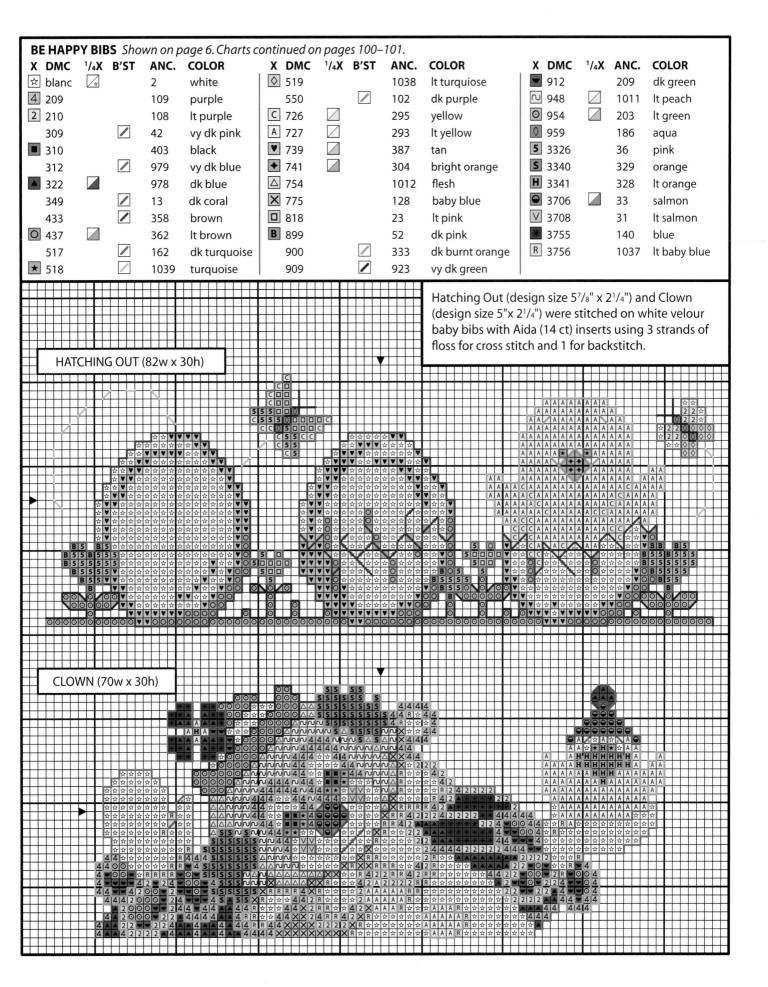

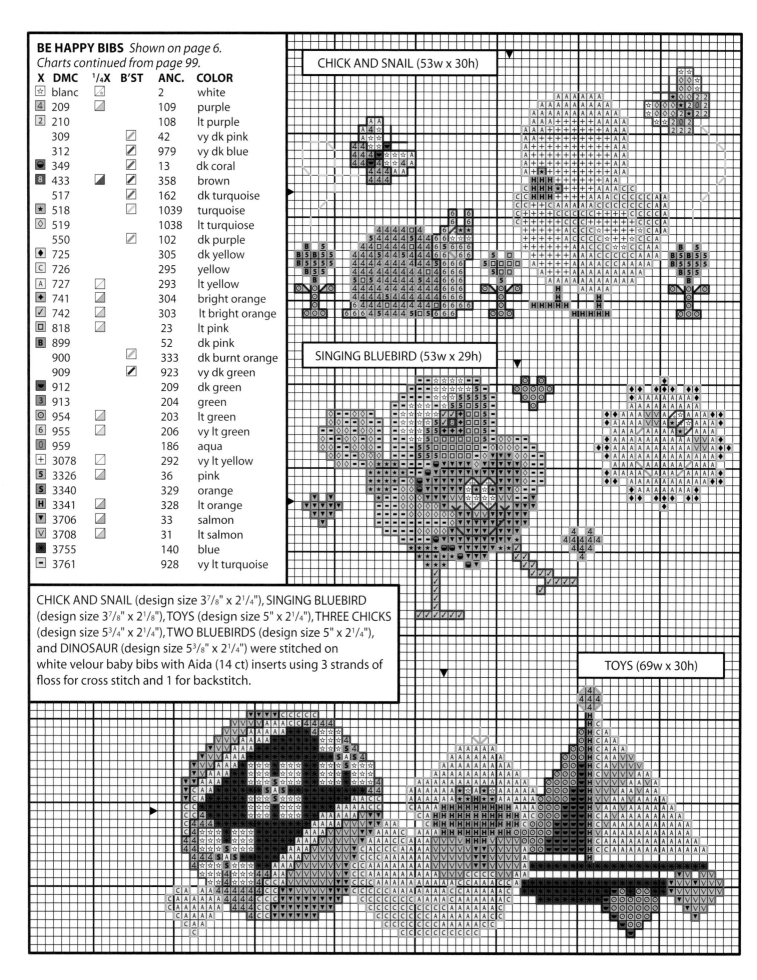

BE HAPPY BIBS Shown on page 6.
Charts continued from page 99.

X	DMC	¼X	B'ST	ANC.	COLOR
☆	blanc			2	white
4	209			109	purple
2	210			108	lt purple
	309		✎	42	vy dk pink
	312		✎	979	vy dk blue
◑	349		✎	13	dk coral
8	433	◨	✎	358	brown
	517		✎	162	dk turquoise
★	518			1039	turquoise
◇	519			1038	lt turquoise
	550		✎	102	dk purple
◆	725			305	dk yellow
C	726			295	yellow
A	727	▱		293	lt yellow
✦	741	▱		304	bright orange
✓	742	▱		303	lt bright orange
▢	818	▱		23	lt pink
B	899			52	dk pink
	900		✎	333	dk burnt orange
	909		✎	923	vy dk green
▬	912			209	dk green
3	913			204	green
◉	954	▱		203	lt green
6	955	▱		206	vy lt green
0	959			186	aqua
+	3078	▱		292	vy lt yellow
5	3326	▱		36	pink
S	3340			329	orange
H	3341	▱		328	lt orange
▼	3706	▱		33	salmon
V	3708	▱		31	lt salmon
✳	3755			140	blue
▬	3761			928	vy lt turquoise

CHICK AND SNAIL (53w x 30h)

SINGING BLUEBIRD (53w x 29h)

CHICK AND SNAIL (design size 3⅞" x 2¼"), SINGING BLUEBIRD (design size 3⅞" x 2⅛"), TOYS (design size 5" x 2¼"), THREE CHICKS (design size 5¾" x 2¼"), TWO BLUEBIRDS (design size 5" x 2¼"), and DINOSAUR (design size 5⅜" x 2¼") were stitched on white velour baby bibs with Aida (14 ct) inserts using 3 strands of floss for cross stitch and 1 for backstitch.

TOYS (69w x 30h)

THREE CHICKS (79w x 30h)

TWO BLUEBIRDS (69w x 30h)

DINOSAUR (74w x30h)

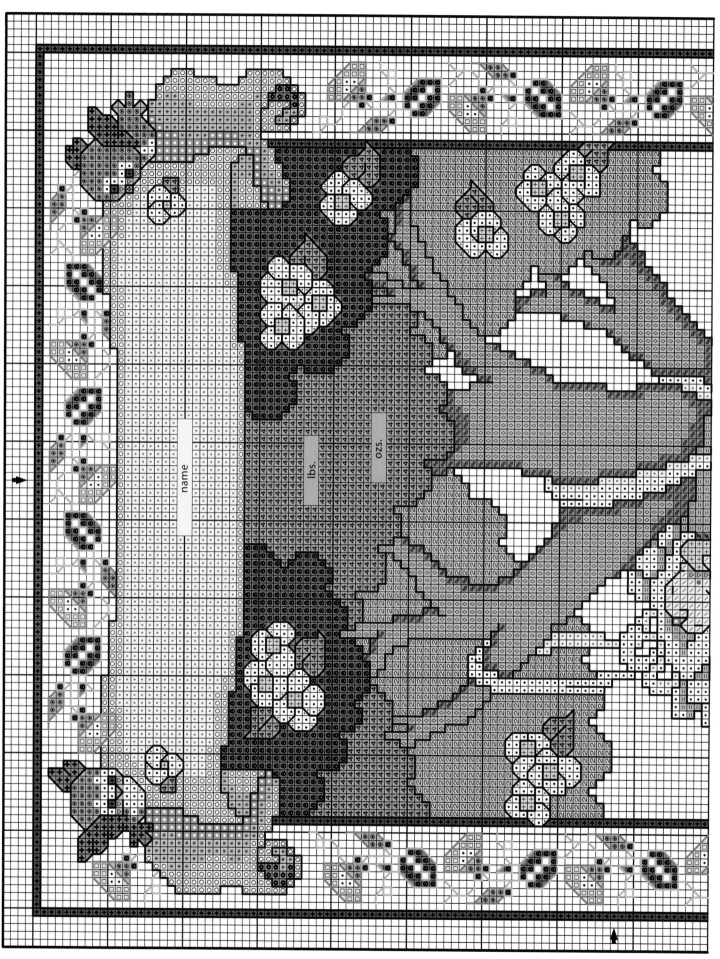

name

lbs.

ozs.

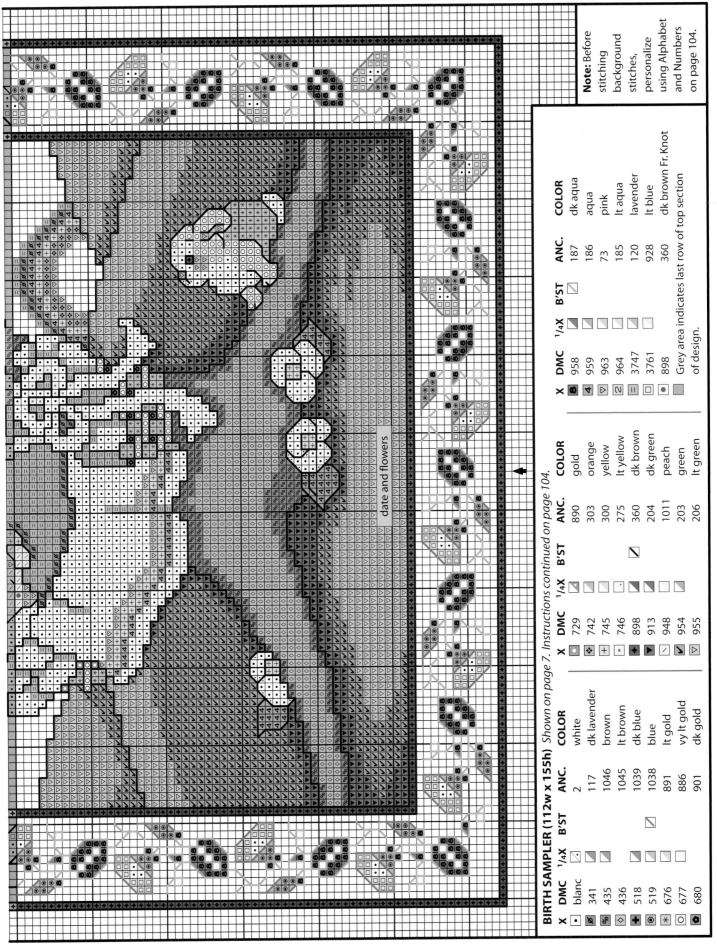

BIRTH SAMPLER (112w x 155h) *Shown on page 7. Instructions continued on page 104.*

date and flowers

Instructions continued on page 104.

X	DMC	1/4X	B'ST	ANC.	COLOR
•	blanc			2	white
∅	341			117	dk lavender
%	435			1046	brown
◇	436			1045	lt brown
✚	518			1039	dk blue
◉	519			1038	blue
✳	676			891	lt gold
○	677			886	vy lt gold
◓	680			901	dk gold

X	DMC	1/4X	B'ST	ANC.	COLOR
◔	729			890	gold
❖	742			303	orange
✛	745			300	yellow
⊡	746			275	lt yellow
✦	898		◥	360	dk brown
▶	913			204	dk green
╱	948			1011	peach
↵	954			203	green
▷	955			206	lt green

X	DMC	1/4X	B'ST	ANC.	COLOR
◧	958	◣	◢	187	dk aqua
4	959	◣		186	aqua
▷	963	◣		73	pink
▨	964	◣		185	lt aqua
‖	3747	◣		120	lavender
□	3761	□		928	lt blue
●	898	◩		360	dk brown Fr. Knot
		▨			Grey area indicates last row of top section of design.

Note: Before stitching background stitches, personalize using Alphabet and Numbers on page 104.

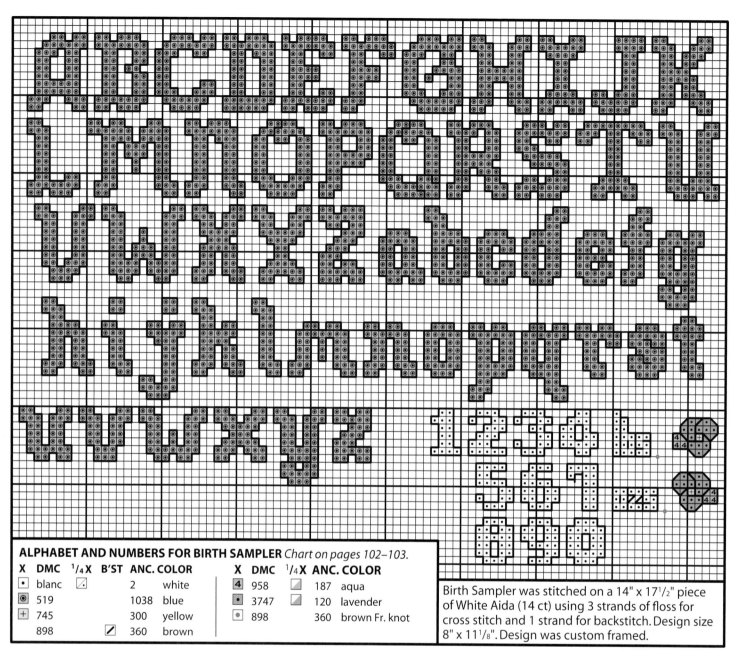

ALPHABET AND NUMBERS FOR BIRTH SAMPLER *Chart on pages 102–103.*

X	DMC	¼X	B'ST	ANC.	COLOR	X	DMC	¼X	ANC.	COLOR
•	blanc	◩		2	white	4	958	◪	187	aqua
◉	519			1038	blue	•	3747	◪	120	lavender
+	745			300	yellow	◉	898		360	brown Fr. knot
	898		◹	360	brown					

Birth Sampler was stitched on a 14" x 17½" piece of White Aida (14 ct) using 3 strands of floss for cross stitch and 1 strand for backstitch. Design size 8" x 11⅛". Design was custom framed.

Birth Certificate was stitched on a 15" x 15" piece of White Aida (14 ct) using 3 strands of floss for cross stitch and 1 strand for backstitch. Use alphabet and numbers shown on right to personalize Certificate. Design size 7¼" x 7¼", excluding footprints. Design was custom framed.

Place footprints before stitching. To make footprint template, cut a 15" square of tracing paper. Measure 4" from center bottom of tracing paper and mark with a pencil. Matching marking on tracing paper to center bottom of charted design, place tracing paper over chart; trace solid grey lines. Cut template along traced lines. Matching edges, pin template to fabric. Pour approximately 1 teaspoon acrylic paint onto paper plate; add a couple of drops of water to paint and stir with toothpick. Dab sponge brush into thinned paint; use brush to lightly paint bottom of baby's foot. Gently press foot onto fabric within cut out area of template. Repeat for remaining footprint.

ALPHABET AND NUMBERS FOR BIRTH CERTIFICATE

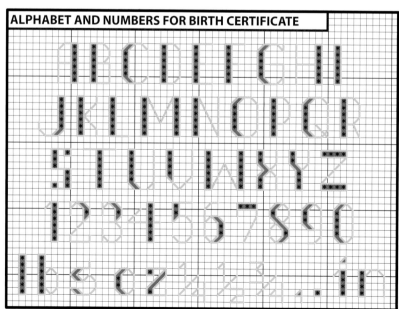

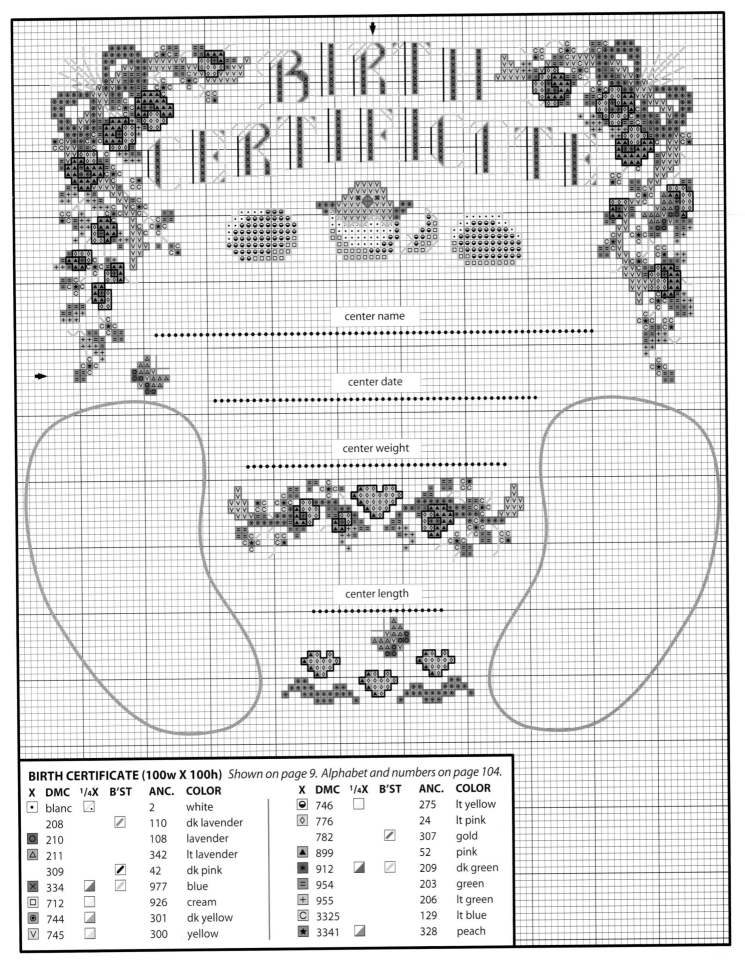

center name

center date

center weight

center length

BIRTH CERTIFICATE (100w X 100h) *Shown on page 9. Alphabet and numbers on page 104.*

X	DMC	1/4X	B'ST	ANC.	COLOR		X	DMC	1/4X	B'ST	ANC.	COLOR
•	blanc	◿		2	white		◖	746	☐		275	lt yellow
	208		◿	110	dk lavender		◇	776			24	lt pink
◉	210			108	lavender			782		◿	307	gold
△	211			342	lt lavender		▲	899			52	pink
	309		◿	42	dk pink		✳	912	◪	◿	209	dk green
✕	334	◪	◿	977	blue		=	954			203	green
☐	712	☐		926	cream		+	955			206	lt green
◉	744	◪		301	dk yellow		C	3325			129	lt blue
V	745	◿		300	yellow		★	3341	◪		328	peach

Birdbath was stitched on White Aida (14 ct) using 3 strands of floss for cross stitch and 1 strand for backstitch. Design size 5⅞" x 6⅞". See Tote Bag Finishing, page 111.

BIRDBATH (81w x 96h) *Shown on page 7.*

X	DMC	¼X	B'ST	ANC.	COLOR	X	DMC	¼X	B'ST	ANC.	COLOR	X	DMC	¼X	ANC.	COLOR
·	blanc			2	white	❖	742			303	orange	⑧	958		187	dk aqua
✚	518			1039	dk blue	＋	745			300	yellow	4	959		186	aqua
◉	519			1038	blue	◆	898			360	brown	♡	963		73	pink
⬢	676			891	gold	✔	913			204	green	2	964		185	lt aqua
✳	677			886	lt gold	▽	955			206	lt green	▢	3761		928	lt blue

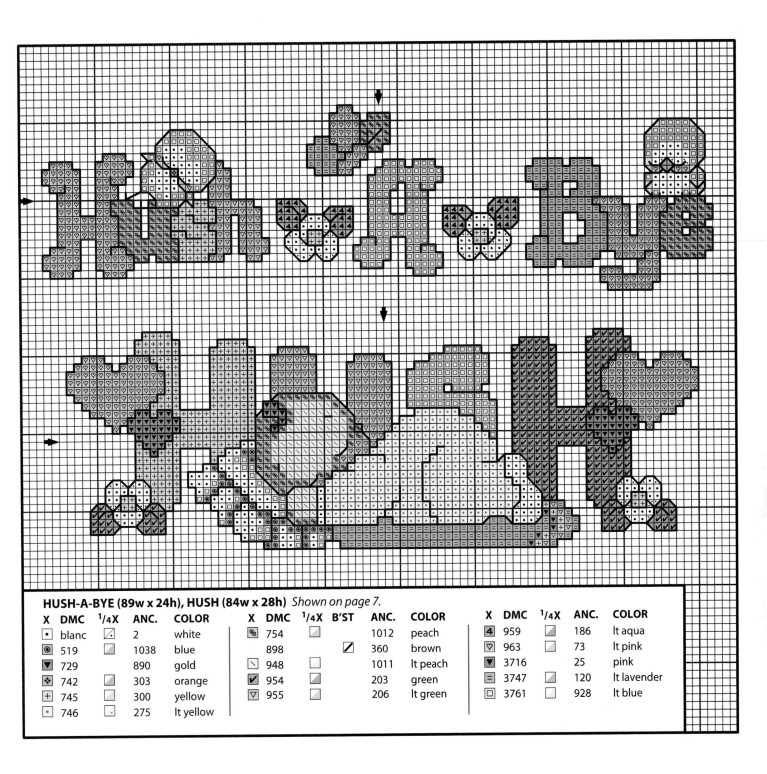

HUSH-A-BYE (89w x 24h), HUSH (84w x 28h) *Shown on page 7.*

X	DMC	¼X	ANC.	COLOR		X	DMC	¼X	B'ST	ANC.	COLOR		X	DMC	¼X	ANC.	COLOR
•	blanc		2	white		%	754			1012	peach		4	959		186	lt aqua
⊙	519		1038	blue			898		∕	360	brown		▽	963		73	lt pink
▼	729		890	gold		⬆	948			1011	lt peach		▼	3716		25	pink
❖	742		303	orange		✔	954			203	green		=	3747		120	lt lavender
+	745		300	yellow		▽	955			206	lt green		▢	3761		928	lt blue
•	746		275	lt yellow													

Hush-a-bye was stitched on a baby bib with Aida insert (14 ct) using 3 strands of floss for cross stitch and 1 strand for backstitch. Design size 6³/₈" x 1³/₄".

Hush was stitched on a 12" x 8" piece of White Aida (14 ct) using 3 strands of floss for cross stitch and 1 strand for backstitch. Design size 6" x 2".

For door sign, cut mounting board pieces 8³/₄" x 5" and 6³/₄" x 3". Cut batting pieces the same size as mounting board pieces. Centering design, trim stitched piece to 9³/₄" x 6". Cut background pieces from fabric 11³/₄" x 8" and 8³/₄" x 5".

Center batting and then stitched piece on smaller mounting board piece; smoothly fold and glue fabric edges to back of board. Center batting and then larger background fabric piece on remaining mounting board piece; smoothly fold and glue fabric edges to back of board. Center and glue mounted stitched piece onto mounted background fabric.

Glue a 31¹/₂" length of pre-gathered eyelet lace to sign back. Glue ends of a 16" length of ¹/₄"w ribbon to sign back for hanger. Glue remaining fabric piece to sign back. Refer to photo for bow and button embellishment placement.

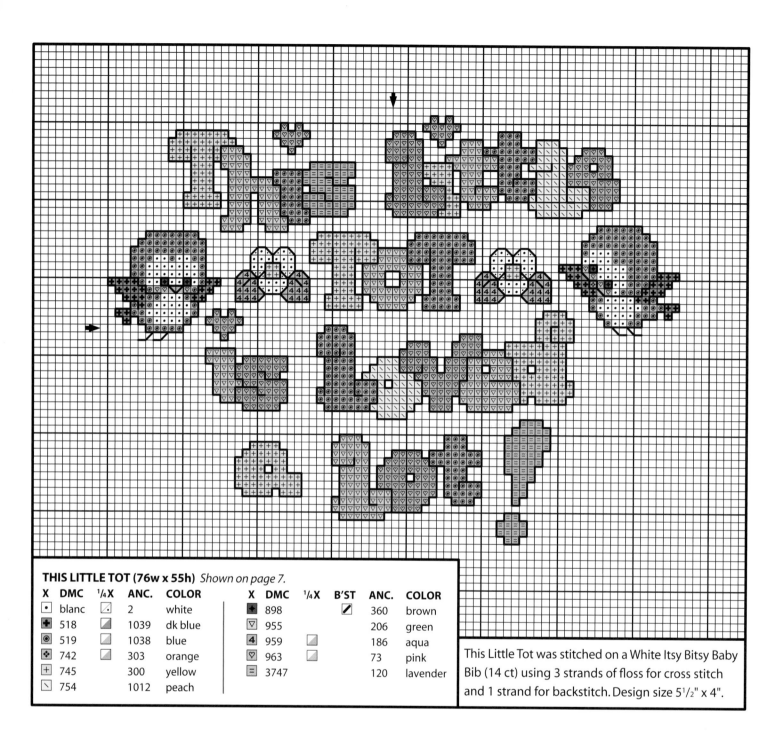

THIS LITTLE TOT (76w x 55h) *Shown on page 7.*

X	DMC	¼X	ANC.	COLOR		X	DMC	¼X	B'ST	ANC.	COLOR
·	blanc		2	white		✚	898		╱	360	brown
✚	518		1039	dk blue		▽	955			206	green
◉	519		1038	blue		4	959			186	aqua
✤	742		303	orange		▽	963			73	pink
+	745		300	yellow		≡	3747			120	lavender
╲	754		1012	peach							

This Little Tot was stitched on a White Itsy Bitsy Baby Bib (14 ct) using 3 strands of floss for cross stitch and 1 strand for backstitch. Design size 5½" x 4".

108

GENERAL INSTRUCTIONS

HOW TO READ CHARTS

Each chart is made up of a key and a gridded design where each square represents a stitch. The symbols in the key tell which floss color to use for each stitch in the chart. Some or all of the following headings and symbols are given for each key.

X – Cross Stitch
DMC – DMC color number
¹/₄X – Quarter Stitch
¹/₂X – Half Cross Stitch
³/₄X – Three-Quarter Stitch
B'ST – Backstitch
ANC. – Anchor color number
COLOR – The name given to the floss color
in this chart

Color Charts

 A square filled with a color and a symbol should be worked as a **cross stitch** or a **half cross stitch** as indicated in color key. The symbol for a **cross stitch** may be omitted or reduced when a **backstitch** crosses its square.

 A triangle should be worked as a **quarter stitch** (or if indicated, a **three-quarter stitch**). In some charts, reduced symbols may be added to color backgrounds.

 A straight line should be worked as a **backstitch**.

 A large dot listed near the end of the key should be worked as a **French knot**.

 An oval listed near the end of the key should be worked as a **lazy daisy stitch**. The chart will indicate the exact size and placement.

Black and White Charts

 A square with a symbol should be worked as a **cross stitch**, or a **half cross stitch** as indicated in color key. The symbol for a **cross stitch** may be reduced when a **backstitch** crosses its square.

 A small symbol in one corner of a square should be worked as a **quarter stitch** (or if indicated, a **three-quarter** stitch).

 A straight line should be worked as a **backstitch**.

 A large dot listed near the end of the key should be worked as a **French knot**.

 An oval listed near the end of the key should be worked as a **lazy daisy stitch**. The chart will indicate the exact size and placement.

HOW TO STITCH

Always work **cross stitches**, **quarter stitches**, **half cross stitches** and **three-quarter stitches** first and then add the **backstitch**, **French knots**, and **lazy daisy stitches**. When stitching, bring threaded needle up at **1** and all **odd** numbers and down at **2** and all **even** numbers, unless otherwise indicated.

Cross stitch (X): For horizontal rows, work stitches in two journeys (**Fig. 1a**). For vertical rows, working top to bottom, complete each stitch as shown (**Fig. 1b**).

Fig. 1a   **Fig. 1b**

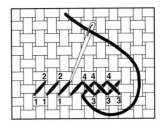   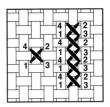

Quarter stitch (¹/₄X) and **three-quarter stitch (³/₄X):** For **quarter-stitch**, come up at 1, then split fabric to go down at 2 (**Fig. 2a**). If working over 2 fabric threads, stitch over one thread and insert needle in hole. For **three-quarter stitch**, continue working and come up at 3 and go down at 4 (**Fig. 2b**).

Fig. 2a   **Fig. 2b**

    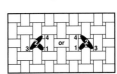

Half cross stitch (¹/₂X): This stitch is one journey of the **cross stitch** and is worked from lower left to upper right as shown in **Fig. 3**.

Fig. 3

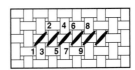

Backstitch (B'ST): For outlines and details, **backstitch** should be worked after the design has been completed (**Fig. 4**).

Fig. 4

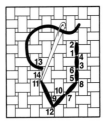

French knot: Bring needle up at 1. Wrap floss once around needle. Insert needle at 2, tighten knot, and pull needle through fabric, holding floss until it must be released (**Fig. 5**). For a larger knot, use more floss strands; wrap only once.

Fig. 5

Lazy daisy stitch: Bring needle up at 1 and make a loop. Go down at 1 and come up at 2, keeping floss below point of needle (**Fig. 6**). Pull needle through and go down at 3 to anchor loop, completing stitch.

Fig. 6

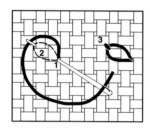

WORKING OVER TWO FABRIC THREADS

When working over two fabric threads, the stitches should be placed so that the vertical fabric threads support each stitch. Make sure that the first cross stitch is placed on the fabric with stitch 1–2 beginning and ending where a vertical fabric thread crosses over a horizontal fabric thread (**Fig. 7**).

Fig. 7

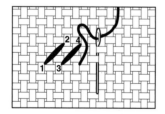

WORKING ON WASTE CANVAS

Cut canvas 2" larger than design; baste to garment. To give a firmer stitching base when working on knit fabric, cut a piece of lightweight interfacing 2" larger than hoop and baste to wrong side of fabric. Place garment in hoop; work design using a sharp needle. Trim canvas to within ³/₄" of design. Dampen canvas slightly to remove sizing. Use tweezers to pull out canvas threads one at a time. Trim interfacing close to design.

HOW TO DETERMINE FINISHED SIZE

The finished size of your design will depend on the **thread count per inch** of the fabric being used. To determine the finished size of the design on any fabric, divide the number of squares (stitches) in the width of the charted design by the thread count of the fabric. For example, a charted design with a width of 80 squares worked on 14 count Aida will yield a design 5³/₄" wide. Repeat for the number of squares (stitches) in the height of the design. (**Note:** *To work over two fabric threads, divide the number of squares by one-half the thread count.*) Then add the amount of background fabric you want plus a generous amount for finishing. It is better to waste a little fabric than to come up short.

USING THE RIGHT NUMBER OF FLOSS STRANDS

Project instructions usually include the number of floss strands to use. If using a different fabric or working with an alphabet, the table below provides suggested number of floss strands for common fabric thread counts.

Thread Count per Inch	Number of Strands for Cross Stitch	Number of Strands for Backstitch	Number of Strands for French Knot
8.5	6	2	4
10 or 11	4 or 5	2	3
12 or 13	3	1	2
14	2 or 3	1	1 or 2
16	2	1	1
18	2	1	1
22	1	1	1

FINISHING INSTRUCTIONS

Stiffened Design Finishing

Cut a piece of cotton fabric for backing the same size as stitched piece. Apply fabric stiffener to back of stitched piece. Matching wrong sides, place stitched piece on backing fabric; allow to dry. Apply stiffener to back of stiffened design. When dry, trim to 1 square from edges of design. To prevent fraying, apply a small amount of stiffener to trimmed edges.

For Large Candy Corn button cover, glue button cover to back of stiffened Large Candy Corn.

For Witch necklace, refer to photo to attach jump rings to stiffened Witch and Large Candy Corn. String plastic beads and stiffened designs on satin cord. To prevent beads from sliding, knot cord close to end beads. Tie necklace at desired length. Knot ends; trim excess cord.

Jar Lid Finishing

Using flat piece of lid for pattern, cut a circle from adhesive mounting board. Using opening of screw ring for pattern, cut a circle of batting. Center batting on adhesive side of board; press into place. Center stitched piece on board and press edges onto adhesive. Trim edges close to board. Glue board inside screw ring. Decorate jar as desired.

Mug Finishing

Using a purchased snap together mug with a Vinyl-Weave™ (14 ct) insert, stitch design at right end of vinyl if mug is to be used by a right-handed person and at left end of vinyl for a left-handed person. After stitching, place insert in mug with short ends of vinyl aligned with handle. Remove stitched piece before washing mug.

Tote Bag Finishing

Note: When sewing, match right sides and raw edges and use a 1/2" seam allowance unless otherwise indicated.

1. Centering design, trim stitched piece to $7^1/4$" x $8^1/2$".
2. From tote fabric, cut two $12^1/2$" x $15^1/4$" pieces for front and back, two 3" x 19" pieces for straps, and one $2^1/2$" x $30^1/2$" bias strip for cording. From lining fabric, cut two $12^1/2$" x $15^1/4$" pieces. Also cut one $25^1/2$" length of pre-gathered eyelet lace.
3. To make cording, center $1/4$" diameter cord on wrong side of bias strip. Matching long edges, fold bias strip over cord. Using zipper foot, baste close to cord. Trim seam allowances to $1/2$".
4. Matching raw edges and beginning and ending 3" from ends of cording, use a $1/2$" seam allowance to baste cording to right side of stitched piece. To make turning corners easier, clip seam allowances of cording at stitched piece corners. Remove approximately 3" of seam at one end of cording; fold bias strip away from cord. Trim remaining end of cording so that cord ends meet exactly. Fold end of loose bias strip $1/2$" to wrong side; fold bias strip back over area where ends meet. Baste remainder of cording to stitched piece.
5. Center and pin stitched piece on tote bag front with bottom edge $2^3/4$" from one short edge of tote bag front. Using zipper foot, attach stitched piece, sewing as close as possible to cording and taking care not to catch fabric of stitched piece.
6. For straps, press long edges of one strap fabric piece $1/2$" to wrong side. Matching wrong sides, press strap in half lengthwise. Topstitch $1/8$" from each long edge. Baste ends of strap to top edge of tote front $2^1/4$" from side edges. (**Note**: Be sure strap is not twisted.) Repeat to make and attach second strap to tote back.
7. To form body of tote, sew sides and bottom of tote front and back pieces together. Trim bottom corner seam allowances diagonally and press seam allowances open. Turn tote body right side out.
8. Follow Step 7 to sew lining pieces together, leaving an opening on one side; do not turn lining right side out.
9. Insert tote into lining; sew together top edge of tote and lining pieces. Turn tote right side out through lining opening; press. Slipstitch opening closed.
10. Press one end of eyelet lace $1/4$" to wrong side. Pin lace around tote top edge, overlapping raw end with pressed end. Topstitch $1/8$" from edge through all thicknesses.

Wall Hanging Finishing

Note: When sewing, match right sides and raw edges and use a $1/2$" seam allowance unless otherwise indicated.

1. For center of wall hanging, trim stitched piece to desired size plus $1/2$" on all sides for seam allowances.
2. For inner borders, cut two $2^1/4$"w strips of fabric the same length as top edge of stitched piece. Sew strips to top and bottom edges of stitched piece. Cut two $2^1/4$"w strips of fabric the same length as side edges of stitched piece plus attached strips. Sew to sides edges of stitched piece and attached strips.
3. For middle borders, cut two 3"w strips of fabric the same length as top edge of wall hanging front. Sew to top and bottom edges of front. Cut two 3"w strips of fabric the same length as side edges of wall hanging front plus attached strips. Sew to sides edges of front and attached strips.
4. For outer borders, cut two $1^3/4$"w strips of fabric the same length as top edge of wall hanging front. Sew to top and bottom edges of front. Cut two $1^3/4$"w strips of fabric the same length as side edges of wall hanging front plus attached strips. Sew to side edges of front and attached strips to complete wall hanging front.
5. Cut one piece of backing fabric the same size as wall hanging front and one piece of fusible fleece $1/2$" smaller on all sides than wall hanging front. Center and fuse fleece to wrong side of backing fabric. Sew wall hanging front to backing, leaving an opening for turning. Clip seam allowances diagonally at corners. Turn, press, and slipstitch opening closed.
6. For hanging sleeve, cut a 3"w piece of backing fabric the same width as wall hanging. Press all edges $1/2$" to wrong side. Press short edges $1/2$" to wrong side again and hem. Center and pin hanging sleeve on back of wall hanging $3/4$" from top edge. Slipstitch long edges in place, leaving short ends open for inserting a hanging rod.

Pillow Finishing

Note: You may wish to make a corded pillow; a corded and ruffled pillow; a ruffled pillow; or a corded, lace, and fabric ruffled pillow. Instructions for all of these pillows are below. When sewing, match right sides and raw edges and use a $1/2$" seam allowance unless otherwise indicated.

1. For pillow front, trim stitched piece to desired size plus $1/2$" on all sides for seam allowances. Cut pillow back same size as pillow front.
2. To determine length of cording needed, measure edges of pillow top and add 4". Cut a $2^1/2$"w bias strip the same length as determined measurement. To make cording, center $1/4$" diameter cord on wrong side of bias strip. Matching long edges, fold bias strip over cord. Using zipper foot, baste close to cord. Trim seam allowances to $1/2$".

3. Matching raw edges and beginning and ending 3" from ends of cording, use a $1/2$" seam allowance to baste cording to right side of pillow front. To make turning corners easier, clip seam allowances of cording at pillow front corners. Remove approximately 3" of seam at one end of cording; fold bias strip away from cord. Trim remaining end of cording so that cord ends meet exactly. Fold end of loose bias strip $1/2$" to wrong side; fold bias strip back over area where ends meet. Baste remainder of cording to pillow front.

4. To make a lace ruffle, cut a length of pre-gathered lace the outer dimension of pillow front plus 4". Baste lace to pillow front over cording.

5. To make a ruffle, cut a strip of fabric 5" wide and twice outer dimension of pillow front, piecing as needed. Sew ends of fabric together; press seam allowances open. With wrong sides together, press ruffle in half lengthwise. To gather ruffle, baste $3/8$" and $1/4$" from raw edges. Pull basting threads, gathering ruffle to fit edges of pillow front. Baste ruffle to pillow front over cording or over lace and cording.

6. Use zipper foot to sew pillow front and back together as close as possible to cording, leaving an opening at bottom edge for turning. Trim corners diagonally, turn right side out, and press. Stuff with polyester fiberfill; slipstitch opening closed.

WHERE TO FIND IT

The following products are available at www.TheLeisureBoutique.com
- 14 count Aida
- 18 count Aida
- 22 count Hardanger
- 28 count Linen
- 14 and 18 count bookmarks
- 14 count breadcovers or bread cloths
- Vinyl-Weave™
- waste canvas
- hand towels
- baby bibs
- snap together mugs

The prefinished items listed in project instructions may be found at your local craft store or through online retailers.

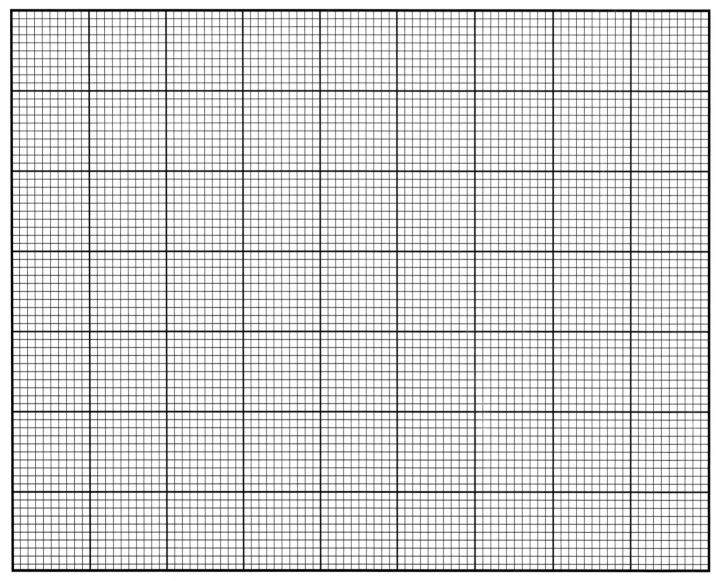

Some fabric provided courtesy of Charles Craft, Inc. and Zweigart®.
Embroidery floss provided courtesy of the DMC Corporation.